Want more of what you've read here?

elisamorg...

Sign up to receive [...]

Book Elisa to speak for your event.

Listen to Elisa on discovertheword.org.

Follow Elisa
on Facebook and Instagram
@ElisaMorganAuthor
and on Twitter
@elisa_morgan.

Elisa Morgan

Really

Living really ... Really living

8. Voskamp, 17.

9. Rohr, *Everything Belongs,* 149.

10. https://en.wikipedia.org/wiki/Coining_(mint).

11. Julian of Norwich, *Showings* (Mahwah, New Jersey: Paulist Press, 1978), 254.

CHAPTER 9: **Our Pivot**—*The Space Between Honest and Abandon*

1. Yancey, 24.

2. Beth Moore, *Praying God's Word: Breaking Free from Spiritual Strongholds* (Nashville: B&H Publishing Group, 2009), 6–7.

3. Eugene Peterson, *The Contemplative Pastor* (Dallas: Word, 1989), 103.

4. Foster, 98.

5. Foster, 27–29.

6. Foster, 70.

7. Louis Evely, *Our Prayer: A New Approach to Everyday Prayer* (New York: Image Books, 1970), 16–17.

8. C. S. Lewis, *George MacDonald: An Anthology* (London: Geoffrey Bles, 1946), 51–52.

CHAPTER 10: **How to Pray the Prayer Coin**

1. Tim Stafford, *Knowing the Face of God* (Grand Rapids, Michigan: Zondervan, 1986), 134.

2. Lewis, *The Weight of Glory* (New York: HarperCollins, 1949) 26.

3. Madame Guyon, *Experiencing God Through Prayer* (New Kensington, Pennsylvania: Whitaker House, 1984), 93.

CHAPTER 11: **Spending the Prayer Coin**

1. Carson, *NIV Zondervan Study Bible,* 1985.

DARING TO PRAY WITH HONEST ABANDON

ELISA MORGAN

Discovery House®
from Our Daily Bread Ministries

"Elisa Morgan's *Prayer Coin* is a powerful exploration of Jesus' two-sided Gethsemane prayer. From 'take this cup' to 'not my will,' this book will pivot you into a more intimate relationship with God."

> MARK BATTERSON, author of the *New York Times* bestseller *The Circle Maker* and lead pastor of National Community Church

• • •

"I love the way Elisa Morgan thinks. She goes deep with her research, wide with her reading, and always brings us back to Scripture. By closely examining and polishing each side of *The Prayer Coin*, Elisa offers us a rare treasure: a book rich with timeless wisdom and practical, you-can-do-this application that could change your prayer life forever."

> LIZ CURTIS HIGGS, author of the bestsellers *31 Proverbs to Light Your Path* and *Bad Girls of the Bible*

• • •

"Elisa Morgan is fearless. Even better, she is honest. With this bravely candid journey, she reframes the timid unwillingness of our faint-hearted praying into the throne-touching, gate-crashing, life-changing intimate surrender that Christ's death provides. It's a stunning reenvisioning of prayer. *The Prayer Coin* is one of her best!"

> PATRICIA RAYBON, author of *I Told the Mountain to Move: Learning to Pray So Things Change*

"Every day, we are faced with difficult and complex decisions, in our personal, family, and work lives. Sometimes we have no idea what the next step should be. Sometimes we know it, but it seems too overwhelming to bear. Elisa Morgan has crafted a profound approach to connecting with God and his resources on this issue, but within a clear, accessible, and simple framework. You will find hope and direction in this material. Highly recommended."

> JOHN TOWNSEND, PhD, *New York Times* bestselling author and founder of Townsend Institute of Leadership and Counseling

. . .

"Elisa Morgan is one of the most passionate, authentic communicators I have ever known. She speaks out of the deepest, most honest places of the soul—and my soul is always the richer—and moved closer to Jesus—for the listening. These are pages I have longed to read."

> ANN VOSKAMP, author of the *New York Times* bestsellers *One Thousand Gifts* and *The Broken Way*

To Evan—

*Thank you for asking me the simple
yet profound question, "Have you ever noticed
that Jesus prayed both 'Take this cup'
and 'Not my will' in one single sentence?
Isn't that powerful?"
In that moment, my understanding
of the Prayer Coin began to form.*

• • •

Contents

• • •

In ancient times, coins were formed through a process of melting valuable metals in an intense heat of over fifteen hundred degrees and pouring the resulting liquid into molds to form round "blanks." Each blank was then sandwiched between a pair of dies with engraved designs.

A coin is "minted" when the blank is struck, or hit with a hammer, forcibly imprinting a different design on each side to create heads and tails (or obverse and reverse, to use more official coin language). While the process is highly automated today, minting of coins still involves striking metal through force to create a two-sided currency.

Prayer is like a two-sided coin, minted in the heat and pressure of life and spent in the bent-knee of practice.

• • •

CHAPTER 1

Our Problems
with Prayer

We are a praying people. We can hardly help ourselves. In a pinch when we need help. Under our breath in a moment of frustration. For loved ones so in need of hope and help. Over our troubled world. After a stunningly happy surprise. We pray.

And yet, we can find prayer baffling. Our tongues grow heavy. Sometimes prayer is just plain scary—after all, what do we say to the God of the universe? At other times, prayer can be unsatisfying. We wonder, Is God listening? Will he answer? Why is he taking so long? Why do we feel so cut off from him? What if we're praying in the wrong way? We look to the Lord's Prayer for guidance. *Our Father, which art in heaven, hallowed be thy name.*

We examine and interpret each phrase. *Thy kingdom come, thy will be done in earth, as it is in heaven.*

We mouth our own prayers after its formula. *Give us*

this day our daily bread. And forgive us our debts, as we forgive our debtors.

We beg God to intervene according to its model. *And lead us not into temptation, but deliver us from evil.*

We memorize it. *For thine is the kingdom, and the power, and the glory, for ever.*

A clear prayer formula, right? No doubt. And helpful for all who long to connect with God in spiritual conversation. After all, Jesus offered the model in response to the disciples' plea, "Teach us to pray" (Luke 11:1). In Matthew 6:9, Jesus says plainly, "This, then, is how you should pray."

That should work, then, right?

But sometimes it doesn't seem to.

In his Sermon on the Mount, Jesus beckons us, saying, "Ask and it will be given to you" (Matthew 7:7). So we do. Sometimes we receive. In other moments, we stand gapingly empty.

In Luke 18:1, Jesus "told his disciples a parable to show them they should always pray and not give up." We ratchet up our efforts with consistency and sincerity. Sometimes we see results. Sometimes we don't.

Ugh.

Author Paul Miller commiserates, "Our inability to pray comes from the Fall. Evil has marred the image. We want to talk to God but can't. The friction of our desire to pray, combined with our badly damaged prayer antennae, leads to constant frustration. It's as if we've had a stroke."[1]

Oh so true. There are moments I experience a kind

of spiritual aphasia before God. I send commands to my being to express my desires to God and my yieldedness to his will but my then mouth won't move. James writes of the trouble such a condition can bring, "You do not have because you do not ask" (James 4:2).

Maybe I'm a doubter, "like a wave of the sea, blown and tossed by the wind" (James 1:6). James goes on to say that such a person "should not expect to receive anything from the Lord" (verse 7).

Or maybe I'm too selfish to experience God's response to my prayers as James, again, warns, "When you ask, you do not receive, because you ask with wrong motives, that you may spend what you get on your pleasures" (James 4:3).

Oh my . . . what to do? Pray more?

It's not that I don't pray. I pray constantly, in an unending babbling before God. And I've come to understand that this ongoing conversation actually "counts"— it's even considered the real definition of a life of prayer. The psalms are filled with examples of David and other pilgrims crying out to God in everyday emotion. Perhaps prayer doesn't have to begin with an "Our Father" and end with an "Amen" to be prayer. Theologian Richard Foster offers me hope as he writes, "Countless people, you see, pray far more than they know. Often they have such a 'stained-glass' image of prayer that they fail to recognize what they are experiencing as prayer and so condemn themselves for not praying."[2]

Whew. Whether bent-kneed and patterned or simply

stream of conscious rumbling, my prayers are just that: prayers.

But I wouldn't really call myself a prayer warrior—surely not like some people I know. I don't have a prayer closet at home. I do have a prayer journal, but between the filled pages yawn un-entered days . . . weeks . . . sometimes even months.

As a twelve-year-old in my home church, I memorized the Lord's Prayer, but I don't often recite it. I ask, but I don't always receive. I try to pray and never give up. Really, I do. But sometimes I still forget to pray, and then when I do pray, I sometimes forget what I prayed. I experience—personally—*lots* of prayer problems.

I wonder if there isn't a deeper, more core issue at work here. Nestling down to consider my prayer problems more intentionally, I find myself conflicted in prayer. Pulled in the two directions of what I want and what I think God wants. My will versus his will.

On the one hand, I long to be honest—gut-wrenchingly raw—in blurting out my needs and desires before God and begging him to meet them. *Every single one of them.* But do I dare? Will he hear? Does he care? Will he act? What if he doesn't? Hear. Care. Act. Unsure, I hedge *honest* and dress it up as respectful requests. One inch deep.

On the other hand, I yearn for the courage to abandon my desires in surrender to God's best in all things. But, oh my, what all might "God's best" include? What might he allow? In my life or in the lives of those I love? Uncertain, I wince a compromised yielding.

You relate, don't you?

These are some of the questions and concerns that worm their way into our prayer closets. We have certain prayer problems. Prayer can become a tug-of-war between our desires and God's. When caught in such a rivalry, we often dig in our heels and settle for repetitious, superficial praying.

Or we might simply stop praying.

Now *that's* a prayer problem.

How can prayer become more satisfying? What can we expect—really expect—when we pray? How can prayer bring us closer to God? How can we come to trust prayer to deliver results? As pastor and author Max Lucado puts it, "We can't even get the cable company to answer us, yet God will? The doctor is too busy, but God isn't? We have our doubts about prayer."[3]

One Sunday morning several years ago, as I was listening a bit robotically to the sermon, my pastor arrowed into my prayer thoughts. "If you always do what you've always done," he said, "you'll always get what you've always gotten."

Do something different in prayer, Elisa.

Okay . . . but what? I kept my eyes and ears open to what "different" might be, with very little result. Was this message from God?

Then help came to me from an unexpected source.

In the deepest hours of Jesus' life on this planet, a two-sided coin of prayer was forged. In the crucible of the garden of Gethsemane, pressed between what he wanted and what the Father wanted, Jesus prayed "Take this cup," and then, "Not my will." His words are recorded in three of the four gospels—Matthew, Mark, and Luke. (They are called the "Synoptics," from Greek words meaning "seeing all together," because they give generally parallel accounts of Jesus' ministry but from the differing perspectives of three different followers). In the fourth gospel, John doesn't actually quote Jesus' prayer but rather illustrates the two sides in the Lord's comments and actions. In all four gospels, they are there. Two sides of Jesus. Two sides of us. Two sides of prayer. The Prayer Coin.

The "pop" in my thinking was palpable. What might I discover about Jesus, God the Father, and myself if I pendulum-swing my prayers between the two sides of the coin? What if I teeter-totter my utterances between what I want and what God wants?

I pause to let the concept sink in. What, really, is the state of Take This Cup? Perhaps a state of "honest"? An unapologetic verbalization of what is truly within? And what, really, is the condition of Not My Will? I mull over my personal language. *Surrender. Yieldedness. Relinquishment.* Another word has the stickiness needed to stay. A startling word at first (is it even the proper part of speech?), yet here is a word that sums up the surprise necessary to grab my heart: *abandon.* Not as in being abandoned by another. No, abandon as in giving oneself completely over to something. To Someone.

Take This Cup: honest.

Not My Will: abandon.

Two sides of prayer.

I muse over them, wondering which side I pray most

often—and why. What might I be missing by not—at least once in a while—considering the other side, following where it leads?

I've vacillated in my prayer coin, depending on the season. In my earliest prayer postures, as an apprentice in prayer, I chose abandon. Zealously smitten with my new Love, I open-palmed my life before Jesus. I burned with commitment, sizzled with passion, and bubbled with contagion.

Later, likely experiencing burnout, I leaned honest. I cracked open my heart and poured out its contents in unbridled freedom. That I could actually say such things to God! Right in front of God! In his very presence! Honest caught me up into an intimacy that invited me closer and closer to God with more and more of me.

Until, sliding down the curve of honest, I spun back into abandon, freshly aware of my need for grace and forgiveness. Of my other-than-God-ness. Splayed under his authority, I'd discovered yet another facet to honest—something that comes from being honest. God likes me, *loves* me, here. Even—*maybe especially*—in honest.

Somehow I pivot on the edge of honest, straight into abandon.

I see a progression in the process. First, I get more honest with God about what I want. Then I'm more able to embrace his acceptance of me in wanting what I want. Then I'm more and more willing to abandon what I want, since I can believe—truly believe—that what God wants is best. Then, living in abandon, I'm able to be more honest about more levels of what I want, and as a result I'm more able to live in abandon to what he wants. And on and on it goes.

What if I flip-pray this prayer coin, spinning myself between the two sides, one being my desire, the "honest" plea, and the other being the "abandon" of surrendering to his will? All while my relationship with God grows clearer and more and more real?

Surely, I'll never drink the cup that Jesus drank. But what if I kneel with Jesus in his garden prayer, and consider how his ricocheted efforts—between what the human Son wanted and what the divine Father wanted—might become a model of what's available to me in prayer? Might such a practice be "doing more than I've always done and so getting more than I've always gotten?" More honest. More abandon. More . . . intimacy with God.

What if this two-sided prayer coin—daring to pray with honest abandon—could solve my problems with prayer? Take me into the kind of oneness Jesus experienced with his Father? The very intimacy God designed me to enjoy?

So I began a new prayer effort—this prayer coin practice. A "prayer dare" of sorts. An intentional focus on praying the two sides of prayer, as Jesus did in the garden. Honest and abandon. For the issues of prayer that flow from my heart. Some for me. Many for others.

Selecting a new journal, I opened it flat to the first pages, penning on the left side, Take This Cup and on the right, Not My Will. Each entry included the date and my current prayer issue. Take This Cup of _____. I waited and considered. I mulled over Scriptures I'd read just prior. I listed various personal issues, some things I didn't want in my life and hoped God would remove, and some things I yearned for and begged God to provide. Then I moved my hand to the right side of the journal to catalog movement toward Not My Will.

There have been days when my hand hovered, paralyzed, over the blank page. I was unsure how to put honesty on paper. Who would read these words at some point? Would I be unsafely "outed"? Many times, I'd catch myself rotely relinquishing to the right—to Not My Will—and then I'd have to drag my thoughts back to the left-hand, honest side of Take This Cup to reconsider what I really meant. What *were* my feelings and thoughts? What was I truly discovering from God?

From time to time, I've invited others along on this journey. A New Year's Day sermon to my very own church body, laying out the concept and encouraging others to participate. A blog reaching out to readers who might join in. Conversations with family and friends.

And now, you. I'm inviting you now.

You hold the diary of my prayer coin journey. And so much more: A following after Jesus' bowed presence. A searching for peace in God's no-matter-what love and always-present presence. An erupting of genuine hope and perspective in an ever-evolving relationship with God through Jesus. And a possible model for praying that produces all this abundance.

It's not a perfect process. There have been *many* days—even weeks—that I've shoved the coin under piles on the desk of my spiritual formation and returned to my habitual blah-blah praying. But I kept coming back to the coin, praying first one side and then the other again and again, and I think you'll find a sincere effort here. A rumbling, bumbling attempt to move through and beyond the prayer problems that leave me chicken-scratching on the surface of connection with God. And consequently devoid of much of prayer's plunder.

My prayer today is that you, too, will open your heart to the prayer coin concept. That as you express your honest Take This Cup moments to God, you'll find him pivoting your desires in abandon to Not My Will—and that in the process, you will discover an intimacy that crashes you through to a more satisfying relationship with him. The place Jesus came to lead us into.

The Prayer Coin is structured to take you on this journey with me. The chapters alternate in a rhythm between Jesus' model of prayer and our practicing his example.

We'll begin with his pattern of prayer—the intimate communion Jesus enjoyed with his Father throughout his earthly life—a pattern that led him to the two-sided plea. Then we'll see how we can make the prayer coin practice our own.

Next, we'll look at each side of the prayer coin—Jesus' honest and then our honest, Jesus' abandon and then our abandon. Expect to experience a kind of ricocheting between deepened understanding and practical application as we move from Jesus to ourselves, revealing layer after layer of the two sides of the prayer coin.

(Can I ask you a favor here? Hold on with me. This

process is complex. Even if Jesus laid down some of his divine attributes to walk this earth, he is still God—we're not. There's surely a divide between us and our holy God, but the whole point of the gospel is that Jesus came to bridge that gap. I'll do my best to honor the complex revelations of Scripture and their integration in our lives.)

Next, we'll stand at the ultimate pivot point, the "yet" or "but" that allowed Jesus to spin between honest and abandon. And we'll dare to consider our own pivot as well. Here, we'll gather our courage to join Jesus as he reaches across the expanse between God and us.

Finally, we'll move into the prayer coin practice to discover how praying this way can change us and our communities. Together, we'll face the ultimate challenge of the prayer coin: to spend the expensively forged offering lavishly, that it might return to us the abundance it was designed to offer.

These chapters are cumulative, each building on the one previous, stacking our understanding and experience. In the end, I believe, the prayer coin practice offers the power to revolutionize our relationship with God.

If you'd like to go even deeper, the back of the book includes reflection and discussion questions to accompany the video curriculum that is also available to use individually or with a group. In it, you'll find more of my own prayer coin stories as well as the stories of others, like you, who dare to pray both sides and grow deeper in relationship with God.

Okay . . . here we go. Up it flies—the prayer coin—into

the air of discovery. Down it comes. Time for you to make the call. What's it going to be? Honest or abandon? Or . . . both?

• • •

"Prayer is how God gives us so many
of the unimaginable things he has for us.
Indeed, prayer makes it safe for God to give us
many of the things we most desire."
TIM KELLER[4]

CHAPTER 2

Jesus' Two-Sided Prayer

". . . take this cup from me;
yet not my will, but yours be done."
LUKE 22:42

I didn't grow up in a house of prayer. You know, a home where prayers were offered. At bedtime. Over meals. Out loud. At all. I learned to pray as a teenager, modeling my words after the "Lord, we just really pray . . ." versions those older in the faith (but still in youth group) prayed. I grew better at praying as I grew better at knowing God through Jesus—and watching how he prayed.

And wow, did Jesus pray! Not just before meals or during miracles or in moments of crisis as we do. Jesus' prayer life was different. Jesus *lived* prayer. Like breathing, he prayed. Like eating, he prayed. Like sleeping, he prayed. Like walking, talking, moving, and being, Jesus prayed.

Because his time on earth was crafted out of an eternity of unbroken communication with his Father and the Spirit, doesn't it make sense that his prayer on earth was an unbroken flow of communication as well? While Jesus laid aside the free use of his divine attributes and journeyed through the cosmos to take the form of a man (Philippians 2:5–8), his *presence* with the other aspects of his being (God the Father and the Holy Spirit) never shifted. He remained one with them right up to his death on the cross, and then afterwards in resurrection.

When his disciples nudged Jesus to eat after a long day of ministry, he responded, "I have food to eat that you know nothing about" (John 4:32). His prayer focus would match that quoted by Richard Rohr, "Prayer is not 'one of the ten thousand things.' It's *that by which we see* the ten thousand things."[1]

Jesus prayed all the time, punctuating events and decisions with words to his Father:

- He prayed as he was baptized. "And as he was praying, heaven was opened and the Holy Spirit descended on him in bodily form like a dove" (Luke 3:21–22).

- He "often withdrew to lonely [or desolate] places and prayed" (Luke 5:16).

- He prioritized prayer in a no-matter-what inclusiveness. After healing Peter's mother-in-law and then all the sick of the town of Capernaum, "Very early in the morning, while it was still dark, Jesus got up, left the house and went off to a solitary place, where he prayed" (Mark 1:35). After feeding the five thousand plus, Jesus sent the disciples ahead in a boat to the other side of the lake to Bethsaida and then went up on a mountainside to pray (Mark 6:45–46).

- He had deep experiences in prayer at the Transfiguration (Luke 9:29) and when he prayed to be gloried personally and for the well-being of his present and future followers (John 17–18).

For Jesus, prayer was the expression of his union within the Trinity. Prayer was his ongoing conversation with the rest of himself. My pastor likes to use the "Circle of Friends" as an example of the community the Father, Son, and Holy Spirit enjoyed prior to Jesus living on this planet. Perhaps you've seen the clay sculpture of several figures joining arms and facing each other in a circle? Prayer is how Jesus stayed connected within his circle of Being.

Jesus' Garden Prayer

How utterly consistent then that, deep in the darkest night of his life, Jesus crumpled in agonized prayer over the torture set before him. As he prepared for the greatest battle ever to be fought, he called out to his Father for help, wielding the weapon of a single, two-edged sentence.

Winding my way through the gospels of Matthew, Mark, and Luke, my heart twists as I imagine the setting. It's the wee hours of the morning—maybe 1 a.m.—after a long day of Passover celebration and summary teachings offered over the meal. Judas, the betrayer, slinks away to do his deed. The remaining Eleven trudge with Jesus from the upper room, east through the city of Jerusalem and then outside the walls and across the Kidron Valley to arrive at their destination: Gethsemane.

Named for the pressing process in which olives grown on the nearby slopes will be squeezed to release their oil, Gethsemane is a spot familiar to the disciples (Luke 22:39), as Jesus often took them there for private conversation and teaching (John 18:2). Rather than return to Bethany where they had sometimes stayed—likely in the home of siblings Mary, Martha, and Lazarus—on this Passover night Jesus and his team plan to sleep in the garden, within the city limits of Jerusalem in observance of the requirements of Jewish law.[2]

Jesus asks his followers to follow, to watch and to pray against the temptation of *not* following. But the disciples swoon under the weight of a week when Jesus had entered the city atop a donkey, was fanned with palm branches and hailed as King and Messiah. Back and forth between Bethany and Jerusalem they had walked, making the three-mile round-trip journey each day to teach and share in the city and then to rest and be restored together at night.

Then they came to this night, celebrating the Passover together at a table where bread is broken, wine is shared, and words are spoken: "This is my body given for you. . . . This cup is the new covenant in my blood, which is poured out for you" (Luke 22:19–20). Concluding their time with a hymn (tradition tells that Psalms 115–118, were sung after the meal[3]), the disciples journey with Jesus to the garden. At this late hour, their heads buzz with Jesus' words, swirling in a brew with those of the religious leaders and Roman authorities. With their stomachs full from the Passover meal, their eyelids dip and they doze. Weak and without the strength of understanding, their well-meaning spirits slip.

I read on and see Jesus kneeling, face focused upward, the moon's globe spotlighting his sincerity.

Suddenly the scene washes gray, the images blurred by the emotions they evoke. This is no story. No passion play. My mind's eye focuses in on Jesus, the man-God. He no longer kneels in haloed holiness but buckles to the dirt, cheek smeared with mud, nose grazed against the cold of a stone, fingernails tearing at the soil, body recoiling into the fetal shape he once occupied within the womb of a woman.

And here, pressed down in a garden, Jesus lifts the prayer coin: "Take this cup from me; yet not my will, but yours be done" (Luke 22:42).

I draw back to watch, peeking through my fingers, as if turning my full attention to him would somehow make this moment more real than I can bear. I thought I knew this Holy Week happening. This chapter and verse. This necessary part of the whole . . . of the holy. But do I?

I know well, oh so many moments along the way of his suffering, gratefully accessing the deliverance they offer my very being. I've familiarly focused in on Jesus in the upper room, offering his body and blood and I remember, as instructed, each time I partake of communion: "This is my blood of the covenant, which is poured out for many" (Mark 14:24); "This is my body given for you; do this in remembrance of me" (Luke 22:19). I've journeyed through his words in the book of John, chapter after chapter of his prayer—for his own glorification, for his disciples, for his future followers, including me and you. I've mouthed his words over my community of believers: Make us one—"just as you are in me and I am in you" (John 17:21). From the foot of the unavoidable cross I've heard him punctuating heaven, uttering his final human prayer: "My God, my God, why have you forsaken me?" (Matthew 27:46). I deeply love Jesus for enduring this for me. What I deserve. I realize that my hand helped place the nail, and I hear him pray, "Forgive them, for they do not know what they are doing" (Luke 23:34). And when he cries, "It is finished" (John 19:30), I stretch my gaze forward to when it is, finally . . . finished, and I am released to be what I was made to be. When we all are. Yet because Jesus gave his life in this horrific gesture of love, I am convinced that even *now*, in light of what he has already completed, I can live differently.

Each cross station has changed me—from lost to found, from imprisoned to freed, from blind to seeing and deaf to hearing.

But am I wholly found, fully free? Do I see? Do I hear?

Turning about, back to his garden prayer in Gethsemane, I wonder, *Have I ever settled in* this *part of the story?* This three-hour window referred to as "the sanctuary of the sorrow of Jesus' soul."[4] Have I deeply considered the torturous, inevitable tug-of-war that led to his eventual sacrifice for me? Have I braked hard and bent my being next to him, turning my ear to his plea? Have I placed my arms around his heaving shoulders, tucked his head into my neck, and held the need of his heart in my own? Have I risked slicing my own heart open with his two-edged prayer? Have I let Jesus be who he was, where he was, how he was in that moment?

Have I *entered* into Jesus' garden prayer?

Jesus' Two-Sided Prayer

Two opposite pleas pierce Jesus' final night on earth before the Father. On the one hand, he leans human. On the other, he surrenders divine. That he does both at once is stunning. That there is a record of his doing so—for us to witness and, maybe, model—leaves me tongue-tied.

How did Jesus pray both sides of prayer? How could he say both "no" and "yes" in a single supplication? Such a braided duality. Take This Cup. Not My Will. And *why* would he? Fully God, why would he need to request the removal of something he knew he would ultimately triumph over?

While preparing for a funeral, pastor Max Lucado opened his Bible to review the two texts the family had requested. On one side he located Psalm 23:1, "The LORD is my shepherd, I lack nothing." He began to flip backward to the second passage and realized it was on the same open page, just left of the Scripture he'd been considering. Psalm 22:1 read, "My God, my God, why have you forsaken me?" Lucado was surprised to see both Scriptures—two glaringly opposite sentiments— staring at him from opposite pages of his open Bible.[5]

Oh the whiplash of the psalms! And both of these specific prayers penned by David! One man offering two diverse expressions. Is it possible that these two seemingly opposite sides of prayer, of need, of reality, are wedded for good reason? How might our faith be strengthened if we embrace their link in the life of Jesus? In his final night of preparation for his final act of love? In our lives as well?

Mashed together in Jesus' two-sided request are two opposite prayers. One is a vulnerable plea to avoid the suffering of the cross, made to the Sovereign One who was fully capable of coming up with another solution. The second prayer is a whole understanding that Jesus' ultimate purpose on earth was to provide a way out of our predicament of sin. He freely said, "This is what I want," (or really, what I *don't* want), while also uttering, "But what do you want, Father?" Jesus' prayer coin expression unapologetically illustrates the "both-and" kind of relationship he experienced with his Father.

Jesus prayed both sides of the prayer coin. Honest and abandon.

Both. And. And more.

In the first garden, humankind was created to enjoy ongoing communion with God—but we chose disobedience and broke off our relationship with our Maker. In the second garden, the God-man modeled for us an intimate prayer of connection. Today, when we embrace and believe the redemption Jesus accomplished for us on the cross, might we go further to enjoy a restored relation-ship—the full intimacy Jesus has with the Father? The "both, and, and more" relationship he died to resurrect?

Jesus' Invitation

Slow, now.

Can you go there? To the garden? Consider . . . in his hours of desperation in the garden, Jesus invites *participation* in his prayer. As he pours out his heart to the Father, he taps his disciples to accompany him. To stay with him. To keep watch with him. Eventually, to pray for themselves against the temptation they would face. To listen to him as he prays the most anguished prayer of his days on earth. Take This Cup. Not My Will. Jesus invited his disciples then . . . and perhaps he invites his disciples now.

In the garden, Jesus invites all the disciples (except of course, Judas) to be with him while he prays. His wording is specific: "Sit here while I go over there and pray" (Matthew 26:36), or, "Sit here while I pray" (Mark 14:32). His request is simple: "Be with me while I pray."

That's it. Just show up and be present. In his first invitation, Jesus is not asking the disciples themselves to pray but rather simply to be with him while he prays his prayer coin. To eyewitness his honest and his abandon. To observe and absorb his two-sided prayer. Take This Cup. Not My Will.

In the next scene, Jesus separates Peter, James, and John, inviting them even closer. Into his emotions. Into his battle. Into his destiny. Jesus shares with them his devastation at what lies before him, that he is overwhelmed to the point of death. He asks them to stay with him and to keep watch with him—the sense is of an ongoing staying and a continuous watching. An alertness that pushes other matters away to remain present. An enduring state of *being with* Jesus in his need (Matthew 26:37–38; Mark 14:33–34). An *abiding* or *remaining in*, just as Jesus had described in the upper room mere hours before (John 15:1–11).

Why these three—Peter, James, and John? Well, they did form the inner core of Jesus' disciples, the closest of his followers. And each had recently voiced a willingness to go anywhere, do anything with Jesus. Peter had blustered that even if everyone else fell away, he would not—and even if he had to die with Jesus, he would never disown him (Mark 14:29, 31). James and John, meanwhile, had voiced a willingness to drink Jesus' cup themselves (Mark 10:38–39). Maybe Jesus was offering an opportunity to prove their mettle, so to speak, to enact their pledged allegiance.

Or perhaps it was because these three had been present at the Transfiguration (see Matthew 17:1–2), and were therefore somehow prepared to witness Jesus' agony.

We can't say for sure. But Jesus invites these closest of his followers even closer. He pings the invitation to the inboxes of their beings because he needs them here for himself. He is human, after all, and he longs to siphon their meager faith fuel as he faces his Father's abandonment. Might this frail band of brothers stay with Jesus when all others betray? Could there be even a few of the few to comprehend the ordeal before him, acknowledging his suffering even as he comes to its entrance? He needs another Mary of Bethany, offering a gesture of love he can carry with him through his suffering (Mark 14:1–9).[6]

Jesus also needs the disciples here for themselves—to prepare them for all they will face in the future, both with and without him. In this last laboratory of learning, Jesus prepares a final lesson of dependency. He will act out the torture of following the Father, no matter what the cost. He will demonstrate the exorbitant cost of the love—both given and received—that he has with his Father. In doing so, Jesus will mirror what the disciples too can possess.

He's known this hour would come. He's dreaded it, and he's wedded his very being to it. Now he extends the invitation for his beloved to join him as he rounds the corner from preparing to daring. An opportunity to enter into the intimacy he was destined to die to provide.

But Peter, James, and John decline. Bowing under exhaustion—of the grief slowly falling on them and the physical depletion of long, long days and nights—they sleep (Luke 22:45). No sitting. No staying. No watching. When Jesus returns to draw fresh hope and energy from their presence, he finds them slumbering like weary puppies in a pile. So dear to his heart but such little help to his soul.

Now Jesus makes a final invitation, asking his

followers to pray. The focus of the prayer Jesus directs is that they don't fall into temptation (Matthew 26:41; Mark 14:38; Luke 22:40). His all-seeing eyes scan the next hours, days, and weeks, anticipating the struggles that so many of his disciples will encounter. Peter's denial. Thomas's doubt. Mary Magdalene's bitter grief. The anguish that undoubtedly racked John, "the disciple whom Jesus loved" (John 13:23), as he raced to the empty tomb (John 20:1–4). The disorientation of the disciples on the road to Emmaus. His vision stretches out to their life spans and to the future of *all* believers in the distance. Will anyone witness and record, much less experience, what could be a pivotal prayer practice for his followers?

Luke reports that at some point Jesus withdraws further, "about a stone's throw" (Luke 22:41), several yards beyond the disciples. Death is truly a solitary journey. Jesus' isolated death made it possible for God to go with us in ours. Because he was alone, we never will be.

Three times Jesus asks his disciples to join him— because he needs them here for himself and because he needs them here for themselves. And three times, the disciples disappoint. When Jesus returns from his painful prayer vigil only to find the disciples asleep again, his response includes understanding of and compassion for their human ordeal of bodily and spiritual exhaustion (Matthew 26:41–43; Mark 14:37–41; Luke 22:45–46) as well as a level of exasperation (Matthew 26:40). Could they not have stayed awake just one hour? They have no response (Mark 14:40).

To be fair, it appears that in some way the disciples actually did absorb Jesus' garden prayer. While they may not have embraced his weary body or wiped his brow or offered sips of spiritual sustenance, they did give us the prayer that you and I study today. Perhaps Peter, James, and John actually listened in as Jesus prayed these words. Or maybe Jesus included this prayer coin in his forty-day ministry between the resurrection and the ascension (Acts 1:1–3). Though we can't say exactly how and where it happened, someone in the bunch heard and saw with some part of their being and recorded the prayer for the church. Likely several "someones," each from their own perspective: certainly Matthew, Peter (who many believed provided details for Mark's gospel), and others present who were interviewed by Luke.

We have to wonder, would their participation that night have made a difference to Jesus? To their own faith? To the course of Christianity?

Go further.

Jesus invited his disciples then . . . and he invites his disciples now. You and I are invited to participate. We've always been included in Jesus' invitation to intimacy. Why not follow our ultimate Model in all things— even here? As twenty-first century disciples, what if we accept the invitation declined by the first century's first followers?

My prayer antennae twitch at the thought. Perhaps here is a two-sided practice that speaks solutions into our prayer problems—both for those of us experienced in prayer yet still wanting more and for those of us unacquainted with the practice at all. Here is a model for our personal decision-making moments. A way through crisis. An on-ramp to intimacy that assures us we are not alone. An everyday tool for the forging of an unbroken relationship with the God who made us to be one with him.

• • •

"For the happy man prayer is only a jumble of words, until the day when sorrow comes to explain to him the sublime language by means of which he speaks to God."
ALEXANDRE DUMAS[7]

• • •

"Last week I found out from my oncologist that my cancer was now getting more aggressive and the prognosis was not good. I was struggling with how to pray. Then Saturday I felt I heard God speaking, 'Pray like my Son did with both honesty and abandon.' Since then I've been trying to pray like that each day."
GARY

CHAPTER 3

Our Two-Sided Prayer

". . . take this cup from me;
yet not my will, but yours be done."
LUKE 22:42

The calendar on my computer showed, six months out, a purple slash through two weeks in February: OUR DAILY BREAD WOMEN'S CONFERENCE, AUSTRALIA. I hadn't really planned on accepting the invitation to speak for two weekend conferences—too much time and too far away. But when my husband, Evan, a senior leader in the global work of Our Daily Bread Ministries, realized that he'd be going for leadership meetings at the same time, I paused. Together we decided to make the commitment. Besides, in the week between the two events he and I could squeeze in some vacation time alongside the ocean. Sweet!

But in the course of my routine time management, as I scrolled ahead on the calendar, something about that long stretch of purple nudged me to uncertainty. I tried to attend to what it might be, I truly did. But nothing ever clarified, so I trundled ahead, connecting remotely with the team in Australia, preparing talks and Power-Points, arranging for book sales, and planning the five days between conferences as a couple's getaway.

Then in December, a few months before the scheduled trip, Evan discovered the cause of some ankle pain he'd been enduring. A tiny, crazy bone within a tendon in his ankle was broken and he'd require surgery in January—just weeks before we were to leave for Australia.

We paused together again—and prayerfully decided that I would make the trip without him. An eighteen-hour flight shortly after surgery was not a good idea. The doctor spelled out various risks, including blood clots and infection.

I was not super-excited about this solo scenario. Two weeks is a long time to be gone from grandkids, dogs, home, and work responsibilities—and from a recovering husband. But I'd made the commitment, and I'm a stickler for commitments. Evan felt the same way, so we decided I would go alone while he attended his global meetings via Skype.

I chafed against this substitute plan. Why? Oh, lots of reasons. First was the loss of our adventurous couple time, exploring a new country. That was huge! Then I imagined long times with Evan's staff, people I didn't really know—would it be awkward? And staying in an apartment, in a foreign country, with people who were pretty much strangers to me. Oh, and the week between gigs, now that I'd be alone—where would I stay? How would I spend that time?

Honestly, this was a season of life in which I spent a *lot* of time alone due to Evan's travel for work and mine for speaking. In other moments, I would have jumped at the chance for solitude. But not in this one.

Eventually, though, I researched spots along the eastern coast of Australia, sorted through prices, and began to view the in-between time as a mini-retreat. I bent my will toward what seemed clearly to be God's, and he continued the miracle only he could accomplish. He changed my attitude.

So by the time Evan dropped me off at the airport, at 5 p.m. one Thursday in late February, I was actually excited about the adventure before me. Two women's conferences bracketing a five-day beach retreat—*woooooottt!*—I couldn't wait.

I flew from Denver to Los Angeles where I passed a three-hour delay by chatting with Evan, who described the house project he was overseeing as his leg recovered. Finally, sometime around 1 a.m. Pacific, I boarded the long flight for Melbourne where I actually slept a nod or two and arrived a million hours later.

Exiting Arrivals, I prepared to meet my Australian contact, Terry, one of the many local staff members who were new to me. I carefully followed the prompts Evan had outlined to turn off my phone's data roaming—or whatever it was—and access my voicemail, texts, and email. The phone lit up in response. One text from Evan: "Call me when you land and I'll give you an update on my leg." Then, a voicemail from him saying the same thing.

I auto-returned the call and Evan answered. "Hi dear.

Did you land okay? How was your flight?" My intuition zinged off the scale—DANGER! EMERGENCY! ALERT! "What's wrong?" I asked. The tears were already springing up in my eyes as I pulled my enormous two-week suitcase out of the kiss-and-hug mass of other arriving passengers, over to the side of the busy airport hallway.

"Well, I've had a little problem with my leg," Evan answered. "I'm in ICU."

He explained that when he had awakened that morning, just hours after chatting with me, he'd noticed a small red bump on his thigh. The bump quickly spread into an angry splotch that began to seep down toward his knee. Meanwhile, a fever crept up to 102 degrees. All within an hour's time. Evan had called his doctor, who sent him straight to the local emergency room. Now he'd been admitted to intensive care for a serious blood infection. One doctor was talking about amputating my husband's leg. Another asked if Evan had a living will. Did anyone hold his power of attorney?

He was *fine* when I left. And now he was in ICU. I'd been gone for just over twenty-four hours. I *knew* there was a reason for that bothersome doubt about this trip! Here it was.

Evan assured me that he was in the best place possible, and that there was nothing I could do. But my mind zipped through scenarios of how I could get back on the flight I'd just deplaned and head home. With my phone at my ear, I scanned the departure board through a blur of tears. It didn't take much calculating to figure that, due to the turnaround time for international flights, it would require at least thirty hours, and likely more than forty-eight, to return to Denver.

The solid tile of the airport hallway seemed suddenly spongy beneath my feet. I'm sure strangers around me noticed the tears running down my face as I tried to catch my breath and think, but I didn't make eye contact. Shoot, I couldn't have made out anyone's face through the teary mist. I could just imagine what Terry would think, finding me in such a state, his speaker for the next two weeks.

But what to do?

I sniffed back my tears and continued listening to my husband—*my husband in ICU*—reassure me that I was right where I was supposed to be and that he'd be in touch with news as he received it. I told him I'd call the dog-sitter for him. And that I'd contact the kids—our adult, on-the-way-to-being-grown-up kids. I wondered, *How will they respond?* Evan and I promised to talk again in about an hour, after Terry had fetched me and taken me to the place I'd be staying. I punched my phone off.

My will rose up strong. *No!* I felt out of control and frustrated and more than a little panicky. *I do not want this to be happening! I do not want to be thousands of miles away from my husband—tasked with ministering to others—while he could die.*

I blinked blearily at the people towing their suitcases around me, going through life as normal when mine was now anything but. I searched for any sign of Terry.

And I felt God saying to me, *"This is about the kids, Elisa."*

It was just a phrase. And really, it shouldn't have made any sense. But in that moment, it did. Completely. Our kids were then thirty-one and twenty-nine. Both married, one with two kids. They were great human beings whom Evan and I adored. But to this date, *we* had always been the predictable presence in their lives. The ones in charge, meeting *their* needs. To date, they'd never been forced to deal with our mortality. Evan and I had both lost our parents decades prior, and now God was whispering that in some way this crisis would be a balm of ministry for our children. *Watch. . . .*

Okay. Well, sort of okay.

I rummaged through my carry-on for Kleenex, dried my messy, sleep-deprived, now makeup-less face, and peered out through the crowd to see a man who must have been Terry coming toward me.

My Prayer Coin Journal

That January, just three weeks before landing in this multilayered predicament in Australia, I'd begun my prayer coin journal. The canceling of our couple trip Down Under opened a space for me to commit to a thirty-day effort, an attempt to discover what might happen in my heart and life as I dared to pray both sides of Jesus' garden prayer.

The concept had been bubbling up for some time. In fact, I had just preached on it in my church on New Year's Day, inviting the congregation to join me in the experiment. I set up a web page, calling it "A Prayer

Dare," for folks to chart their discoveries so we could all learn from each other.

Stumbling along for several weeks afterward, it became clear to me that I needed a bracketed period to truly experience this practice. With Evan's need to remain home while I traveled abroad—including that gap week and mini-beach-retreat between conferences—I planned a monthlong focus. So on that first day of February I dug out a blank journal I'd been given the prior fall for speaking at a retreat. "Elisa's Prayer Journal," the cover boasted. Its empty pages proved how "active" my prayer journaling had been. Well, I'll be fair: I had another journal where I did write thoughts and feelings and needs and discoveries before God. But this new one was christened a "prayer journal," and as such I hadn't dared crack it open.

Until February 1. On that day, with a sincere commitment, I determined I'd dip my toe into an experiment to help me understand more about Jesus' garden prayer. Across opposing pages, I scribbled Take This Cup atop the left and Not My Will on the right. Each side of Jesus' prayer coin.

Here's where it began:

FEBRUARY 1:

Take This Cup

- My friend's trip to celebrate her sister's fiftieth wedding anniversary—and get back in time for another friend's fiftieth birthday celebration. *Take this cup of anxiety. May you lift the worry she's experiencing regarding traveling through a Denver snowstorm and provide a safe, non-eventful trip out to California and then back the next day. May she be present and represent your faithfulness at both events. May she be able to offer her love language of presence. Take this cup!*

- Another friend's sinking financial situation. *Take this cup of financial crisis. He has done so much to manage his responsibilities! He needs a break. Please provide for his needs.*

- Evan's postsurgical healing [before the infection ordeal]. *Take this cup of injury. I pray for 100 percent healing! May he be restored to doing all the things he needs to do—and all the activities he loves to do too!*

I lifted my pen to the right side of the journal and then looked left to consider each Take This Cup plea. Now what? How could I shift to praying the other side of the prayer coin: Not My Will?

Not My Will

- My friend's trip. *May you turn the unexpected and the interruptions into divine appointments. If she doesn't make it to her destination in time for the anniversary party, or if she's kept from returning in time for the second event, may you give her peace. May she embrace the solitude of travel as you give yourself to her in it. Not my will.*

- My other friend's financial need. *I know that lean times are where we learn. Please reveal your presence through the absence of funds. Be close to him. Help him to see your ability to provide and to recognize that all he has ultimately comes from you. May this time of drought increase his thirst for you.*

- Evan's foot. *The healing process is loooooonnnnng. And the nursing seems unending. But I know that you will use it to shape both of us. Help me to learn as I serve my husband. But what if he still has pain? What if he can't walk well? What if he can't play golf? (That will make his life miserable—and if he's miserable, I will be too!)*

Oops. I realized that I'd slipped back to the left, to the Take This Cup side. I refocused. *I pray both of us will see your presence even in the "nots." Not my will.*

The first day passed. I continued the next.

Take This Cup

- My friend's anniversary trip. *I think she made it . . . haven't heard yet. So I continue to pray that you will use her as your symbol of faithfulness and that you will bring her back safely for the party in Denver tonight. Both are important to her and she wants to be present at both! Take this cup!*

Not My Will

- *Yet keep her or take her where it is* best *for her to be and where you can best use her. You know that place and time. Not my will. (Not hers either.)*

Take This Cup

- My other friend's financial crisis. *He's put his house on the market. Take this cup! He doesn't want to move but he can't see any other way. He might have to file for bankruptcy. He's had the idea of selling a family heirloom, the one thing he inherited from a distant parent. Please provide for him.*

Not My Will

- *Perhaps the idea of selling the heirloom is from you. Could you be using the item he inherited from a parent who ignored him while here on earth to specifically provide for his need? Might this most unlikely source become the exact provision he needs? A touch of tangible love from beyond the grave? Not my will. Help my friend see your provision, your care, and your presence that have always been in his life. Despite the absence of his earthly father, you, his heavenly Father continue to work all things for his good. Not my will.*

Take This Cup

- Evan's foot. *I'm tired. Of bringing more ice and making meals and not sleeping. Of course I love my husband. But, oh, will this ever be over? Take this cup!*

Not My Will

- *You are helping me to understand that you use everything. Everything. You show me that I can't serve in my own strength. I don't have enough. I'm empty. I need you. And you always provide. You surprise me with a night of uninterrupted sleep. An ice machine that makes ice unendingly. Someone brings a meal just when I'm not up to cooking. Not my will . . . not my way but yours.*

Later that month, with the advent of Evan's health crisis and my separation from him in Australia, I upped the ante on my prayer coin journal. I invested for a longer haul, one that would reach beyond that February and into the foreseeable future. On my trip, stunned by the shifting terrain of my life, I pulled out the journal and continued my new prayer coin practice with a sense of desperation.

FEBRUARY 24

Take This Cup

- *I do not want Evan to die! Take this cup of infection.*
- *I don't want to be so far away, and unable to get back home! Take this cup of distance.*
- *I don't want to have to minister and serve others when I'm a mess. Take this cup of responsibility.*
- *I don't want to let others do for Evan what I'm supposed to do. Take this cup of being out of control.*
- *I'm scared! I don't want to be a widow! Take this cup!*

Not My Will

- *I'm here, in Australia, millions of miles away from Denver, for a reason. Help me to see what you are allowing. You seem to be saying that our children need to be involved in this mess. Okay . . . I don't completely get that. They are busy with their own lives and responsibilities. But . . . please, bring our children forward to care for their father. And me? Use me here, I pray. Not my will.*

 The more honest I was, the more open I became to abandon. In fact, as I erupted honest and yielded abandon, I was able to discover more layers to be honest about, resulting in further insights on abandon.

FEBRUARY 24 [LATER THAT SAME DAY]

Take This Cup

- *Please heal Evan. Make him completely better. Take this cup of possible disability!*

- *Might he need ongoing nursing care? I don't think I can provide that. Not now. I have so many commitments. Take this cup of timing. I don't want to provide ongoing, forever nursing care—there, that's more honest. Take this cup of dependency. We're too young for this! Take this cup!*

Not My Will

- *For better or for worse. In sickness and in health. I've always pledged that when illness or even death comes close that I would respond with an attitude of "It's my turn." We will all face diminishment at some point. I am not the exception and neither is Evan. I can see a need to relinquish control today that will strengthen me for whatever is ahead, and whenever it comes. Help me yield. Help me let go and allow what you allow. Not my will.*

An Invitation to Join Jesus

That February, I RSVP'd "yes" to Jesus' invitation to practice his prayer coin, not knowing the crisis Evan and I would be facing just days into the adventure. As I dipped the brush of my heart into journaling my discoveries—both before and after illness seized my husband—I began to see that this two-sided masterpiece of prayer was an invitation to the intimacy Jesus died to provide. I would soon discover that the very same honest and abandon that Jesus prayed before his Father in the most searing crisis of his life was available to me. Because Jesus prayed the prayer coin and found peace to move forward, I could as well.

God places this invaluable prayer coin in the palm of all of our lives. A deliberate inclusion in the four gospels by those who either eyewitnessed or were firsthand told about Jesus. A formative prayer that instructs us even as we utter it, helping us understand and clarify our needs while aligning them to God's best and experiencing his utter embrace of intimacy. An expression of the spirit of Christ that confronts us with our own Gethsemanes and moves us on through our Golgothas and to our own resurrections to God's glory.[1]

Pastor and author Tim Keller suggests there are two purposes of petitionary prayer: to put the world right ("thy kingdom come") and to align our hearts with God ("thy will be done"). He goes on to say, "Neither of these should get the upper hand or our supplications will become either too shrill and frantic or too passive and defeatist. We must make our desires known—and also rest in his wisdom. These elements come back-to-back in the Lord's Prayer, and we also see them together in Jesus' own great prayer in Gethsemane."[2]

Yes. Take this cup. Not my will.

We pray the psalms—a whole book of prayers. We pray the Lord's Prayer. We pray other parts of God's Word. Why not pray Jesus' prayer coin?

Looking back through my journals, I can trace the presence of the prayer coin, even in times I didn't know what it was. I see a record of my own, two-sided prayers, a rippling unwilling willingness.

After a childhood with very little God in it, I plunged myself as a teen into zealously giving all of me over to all I knew of God. I realize now that I've been three-stepping forward and two-stepping back, somehow achieving net gain in my spiritual growth. But now, by the intentional use of the prayer coin, I'm unearthing its amazing treasure.

I continue saying "yes."

• • •

"Most of my struggles in the Christian life circle around the same two themes: why God doesn't act the way we want God to, and why I don't act the way God wants me to. Prayer is the precise point where those themes converge."

PHILIP YANCEY[3]

• • •

"I have been challenged as we have definite human desires and outcomes to request of God. Those have been fairly easy to share with him. But I'm also very aware of God's will and needing to seek that in this and all areas of my life. I'm learning to seek the balance and not see it as either-or."

ELLEN

CHAPTER 4

Jesus' Honest—
Take This Cup

". . . take this cup from me;
yet not my will, but yours be done."
Luke 22:42

Three raw words form a plea punctuated by Jesus' heavy sweat, "like drops of blood falling to the ground" (Luke 22:44). Is there a more honest request than side one of Jesus' garden prayer?

Take This Cup.

Translated: What I want.

It's startling to see this aspect of Jesus. We imagine him all godly, all the time. Not to say he wasn't godly here in side one of his prayer coin—he was, indeed, all godly, all the time. But these three words are so surprisingly human. Take this cup. What I want. They upend us.

How could Jesus actually say such a thing? To God the Father? Take this cup. *My* desire. Didn't Jesus come for this very purpose: to drink the dregs of the dreaded cup, to accomplish the rescue of humankind from the mess we've made?

Just days before, he had foreshadowed this moment. "Now my soul is troubled, and what shall I say? 'Father, save me from this hour'? No, it was for this very reason I came to this hour" (John 12:27). So now he basically says, "Save me from this hour?" (see Mark 14:35) Was he reneging on his end of the deal? Wasn't Jesus' will so tightly braided with that of the godhead that to pull in a different direction would be to split his own three-stranded Being?

We draw back in discomfort at the impossible image of the human Jesus, like an adolescent opposing his Father's orders. No way! That would be sin, right? But Jesus didn't sin! Hebrews 4:15 tells us, "For we do not have a high priest who is unable to empathize with our weaknesses, but we have one who has been tempted in every way, just as we are—yet he did not sin." So how could he choose *for* himself and *against* the Father with such a prayer? How could Jesus hover on the brink of what could only be rebellion? How could he *not* want what the Father wanted? If even for a moment?

As if the request itself isn't bad enough, we also can't help but wonder how Jesus could be so honest in how he expresses it before God. If we dare linger in the physical and emotional context of Jesus' words, we squirm in discomfort. His soul is sorrowful to the point of death. He falls facedown on the ground, the lowliest position for prayer, but also the only position his weary body could accommodate. Some Hebrew references interpret the lament of death as rolling in the dirt (Micah 1:10). As his body stresses to the point that it pushes out great drops of sweat that fall to the ground like blood, our jaws drop. How is that even possible?

It's a lot to take in, isn't it? But it's real, this first side of his two-sided prayer: Take This Cup. Three of the four gospel writers record Jesus' prayer and the fourth writer references it, quoting Jesus saying, "Shall I not drink the cup the Father has given me?" (John 18:11). This extremely unsettling honest side is as real as the second, perhaps more expected, utterance of abandon, Not My Will. In side one of Jesus' garden prayer we find an honest request launched in an honest expression. The most pivotal prayer of Jesus' earthly life began *honest*.

So back to our questions. How could Jesus ask what he asked and do it so honestly? And as we explore Jesus' appeal, what might we discover about the requests we bring to God?

Jesus' Honest Request

Take this cup. The completely human Christ thrusts the very cup of suffering he'd been designed to drink back at the Father.

The "cup" Jesus references is complex. Included in that cup is God the Father allowing Jesus to be hurt with the punishment and judgment that evil warrants (see Job 21:19–20). Your sin. Mine. Our wrong choices. Our selfishness. Our turning against our Creator.

I find it interesting that Old Testament writers often compared God's judgment to drinking a cup filled with an intoxicating beverage, one that would send those who drank it into a confused and disoriented stumbling away from our great God of love. Such a powerful representation of God's final judgment over unbelieving nations, especially for arrogance, for the people who act as if they are able to do life without him (Psalm 75:8, Isaiah 51:17, Jeremiah 25:15). Prophets pointed to the deliverance from sin by a suffering Servant whose death would restore a right relationship between God and his beloved beings (Isaiah 52:13–53:12, 2 Corinthians 5:21, Hebrews 2:10, 5:7–10).

The cup metaphor can also stand for our lives, which can be filled with all kinds of things: certainly good and blessed elements, but also the worst of the worst of our thoughts and choices. The cup of suffering that Jesus would drink would make it possible for another cup to be offered—the cup of life and love and restoration.

- LORD, you alone are my portion and my cup; you make my lot secure (Psalm 16:5).
- You prepare a table before me in the presence of my enemies. You anoint my head with oil; my cup overflows (Psalm 23:5).
- I will lift up the cup of salvation and call on the name of the LORD (Psalm 116:13).
- When we drink the cup of blessing, aren't we taking into ourselves the blood, the very life, of Christ? (1 Corinthians 10:16 MSG)

Oh, the cost of drinking this first cup in order to offer the second! The devastation of draining one to deliver another!

56

No one else could or would be asked to endure such a challenge. When the mother of James and John volunteered her sons to sit at Jesus' right and left in glory, he turned to them with a question: "Can you drink the cup I am going to drink?" (Matthew 20:22). "No problem!" they basically said. To this Jesus replied that they would, indeed, drink *from* the cup, meaning the cup of suffering, as James would be martyred (Acts 12:2) and John exiled (Revelation 1:9). But they could not drink the cup of restoration that only Jesus would drink (Matthew 20:22).

Consider the heart that prayed these three words—Take This Cup—in a garden, alone, just hours before destiny would dawn:

- The royal Son recoiling against the upcoming ridicule, wrongful judgment, and criminal labeling before the world.
- The loyal Son imagining betrayal, desertion, and denial by his most trusted companions.
- The human Son dreading imminent physical torture and crucifixion.
- The perfect, pure, and pleasing Son—who enjoyed limitless favor with his Father—resisting the pain of the Father seeing him as sinful.
- The eternal Son, present before the beginning, anticipating the looming darkness of death, if even for a short time.
- The unendingly connected Son who had left the Father's side but never his heart, railing against the necessary separation in the hours of abandonment

on the cross and the three-day ordeal of death beyond it.

- The heavenly Son descending into the darkness, navigating the hollows of hell.

- The victor Son, who had endured forty days and nights of assaulting temptation in the wilderness, now shackled to his evil enemy in incessant companionship from this moment to the end of the ordeal—much of it without the strengthening presence of his band of followers nor of the power of his triune Being.

The pure insanity of what the Son of God was to endure! The injustice! When we stop to really consider what Jesus was facing, it makes total sense that he prayed, "Take this cup." No wonder he prayed, What *I* want.

Surely the element of temptation played a role here in Jesus' "What I want." Likely, as the Son splayed out his plea, the enemy hissed in response, *"You don't have to go through with this! Save yourself!"*

In such a moment, who wouldn't want to run? Eugene Peterson, in his Bible paraphrase *The Message*, suggests this wording for Matthew 26:39: "My Father, if there's any way, get me out of this."

At the start of his earthly ministry, Jesus had been similarly tempted. Again, Matthew, Mark, and Luke share the scene. It began, as did the temptation in Gethsemane, after an experience of fullness through which Jesus had been prepared. In an overflowing encounter of baptism, the Holy Spirit "descended in bodily form like a dove" and the Father pronounced over him, "You are my Son, whom I love; with you I am well pleased" (Luke 3:22). Then Jesus was filled with Spirit, led by him (meaning guided and carried) into the wilderness. There, Jesus was tempted by the devil (Luke 4:1–2).

And now, after more "full" experiences—the Transfiguration before Peter, James, and John, and then being hailed as King and embraced as Messiah mere days prior—the scales dip. Favor departs and temptation returns.

This second round of attack, in the garden of Gethsemane, echoes the first in the wilderness of the desert in Luke 4:1–13. In both cases, Jesus is alone, and he experiences various entry points of assault:

- *emotional:* In the wilderness, the temptation was to receive authority and splendor by worshiping Satan rather than God. In the garden, the temptation is to forego the shame and separation of the cross by remaining attached to the Father.

- *physical:* In the wilderness the temptation was to break his forty-day fast by making bread from stone. In the garden, the temptation is to avoid the torture of the events leading up to and through the crucifixion.

- *spiritual:* In the wilderness, the temptation was to test God's power by throwing himself off the highest point of the temple. In the garden, the spiritual test would be to abandon his destiny.

After the forty days and nights of Jesus' first temptation, Luke records, "When the devil had finished all this tempting, he left him until an opportune time" (Luke 4:13). Here, in this garden, comes that opportune time. A reboot of the earlier threat. And Jesus knows it. Likely, he has dreaded this full-circle reality. In John 14:30, just hours before this garden scene of temptation, Jesus remarks, "I will not say much more to you, for the prince of this world is coming." Here, in the garden, Satan returns with an onslaught of new trials.

Jesus' response? An honest "Take this cup." *My* desire.

This is *real* temptation experienced by a *real* human being. Jesus was "tempted in every way, just as we are" (Hebrews 4:15).

In his two-sided prayer, is Jesus caving to temptation? Is he reneging on his commitment to save us all? Is he turning from his ultimate purpose?

It's startling to consider, isn't it?

Keep going.

Matthew, Mark, and Luke all underline that Jesus sets up his honest Take This Cup prayer by first acknowledging that God the Father's will ultimately trumps his own. The three gospels differ slightly in their phraseology:

- "My Father, if it is possible" (Matthew 26:39).

- "My Father, if it is not possible . . . unless I drink it" (Matthew 26:42).

- . . . that if possible the hour might pass (Mark 14:35).

- "Abba, Father . . . everything is possible for you" (Mark 14:36).
- "Father, if you are willing" (Luke 22:42).

Everything is possible for you. If you are willing . . . Jesus isn't asking his Father to jettison his redemptive will. Rather, because he knew full well that God *could* do anything, Jesus is asking if there is any other way to accomplish the divine will besides drinking the cup.

I think of the three friends, Shadrach, Meshach, and Abednego, responding to Nebuchadnezzar—would God save them from the king's wrath? "If we are thrown into the blazing furnace," they said, "the God we serve is able to deliver us from it, and he will deliver us from Your Majesty's hand. But even if he does not, we want you to know, Your Majesty, that we will not serve your gods or worship the image of gold you have set up" (Daniel 3:17–18). Jesus, too, purposed to obey God in all things. But Jesus also knew his Father was able to save him. Why not ask?

Did Jesus know what the answer would be? The gospel writers are clear that no one knew the hour—or even the day—of God's eventual redemption of humankind, not the angels and not even the Son (Matthew 24:36; Mark 13:32). It's also clear that Jesus "grew in wisdom" (Luke 2:52) from childhood to adulthood, just as we all do. Yes, Jesus was still God, all-powerful God. But he was also the Son, the completely human Son. A completely human Son would honestly ask.

Now, notice how Jesus prefaces his ask—how he

approaches God. He calls him "Father" (Luke 22:42) or "My Father" (Matthew 26:39). Mark compounds the already surprising familiarity with a double salutation: "*Abba*, Father" (14:36)—today, we might say, "Papa, Father." Jesus precedes his two-sided request just as any Hebrew child would. *Imma* and *Abba* (Mama and Papa) were the first two words Jewish children learned to say,[1] and *Abba* is a tender, folksy term for father, with all formality stripped away.[2] But while a Jewish child would call their father *"Abba"* no Jew would *ever* address God with such a term.[3]

Jesus did.

With a deep knowledge of Scripture, Jesus knew *every* possible name for God: Jehovah, Adonai, El Shaddai, Elohim. Jesus makes an intentionally honest request before his *Abba*. A bold and human request for what he wanted. Take this cup.

Jesus' Honest Expression

Even if we begin to understand how Jesus could ask his Father for such a deviation from divine purpose—Take This Cup—we still stand incredulous at his raw expression. We find Jesus, the God-man, splayed out in the dirt, writhing in agony before his heavenly Father. How could Jesus hurl such honesty?

We wince.

And yet, while Jesus knew he had a purpose to accomplish as God, the fully human Son balked—and he said so to his Father. Honestly.

Layer after layer, the gospel accounts reveal Jesus' multifaceted pain. He was sorrowful and troubled, abandoned by his followers and, on the cross, by his Father. His physical agony included profuse sweating and exhaustion ahead of literal torture. Such intense emotional, mental, and physical pain was expressed in every element of Jesus' prayer.

When he reaches out to his closest companions, urging them to be with him in his agony, they dip under the weight of their own pain. Jesus is left alone with his ordeal. Recent research reveals when a person was alone or holding a stranger's hand while anticipating a shock, the regions of the brain that process danger lit up. But when holding the hand of a trusted person, the brain relaxed. A friend's presence brought comfort and made the pain more bearable.[4]

Though he asked his disciples to stay with him, Jesus endured the agony of the garden alone. The gospel writers communicate emotion through narrative space. Thus, Luke, in describing Jesus withdrawing "about a stone's throw beyond" the disciples (22:41), is emphasizing that from a human point of view, Jesus is truly all alone.[5] For the disciples in this moment, temptation wins and they leave their Lord alone. The only one listening is the One who always listens.

Matthew, Mark, and Luke don't hold back in describing Jesus' state on the eve of his ultimate torture. He is "sorrowful and troubled" (Matthew 26:37) and "deeply distressed and troubled" (Mark 14:33), until he is "overwhelmed with sorrow to the point of death" (Matthew

26:38; Mark 14:34). To be sorrowful in this way is to endure severe mental strain. In the original Greek, this same phrase is used of Herod, who didn't want to behead John the Baptist but couldn't save face before his guests (Mark 6:26); and of the rich young ruler, who went away sad because his great wealth was more important to him than eternal life (Luke 18:23). Such words are rarely used in the New Testament. They are heavy. A heaviness of lead on the spirit. Just reading them, we bow under their weight.

The agony mounts as Jesus' physical body gives way. "And being in anguish he prayed more earnestly, and his sweat was like drops of blood falling to the ground" (Luke 22:44). What? Is Luke saying Jesus was actually sweating blood? Possibly. There is a condition called hematidrosis—a rare condition in a person under extreme stress, in which tiny blood vessels burst and the blood mingles with sweat.[6] In his writings, Aristotle (384–322 BC) mentioned bloody sweat, and many commentators suggest that Luke 22:44 means that Jesus was sweating so profusely, and his body was so stressed, that his sweat drops contained trace elements of blood.[7] Others believe the mention is metaphorical—that Jesus was sweating so intensely that his sweat dripped like clotted blood.[8]

We flip our Bible pages back to the Old Testament and consider David's anguish in the psalms. Such similar language! "Have mercy on me, LORD, for I am faint; heal me, LORD, for my bones are in agony. My soul is in deep anguish. . . . I am worn out from my groaning.

All night long I flood my bed with weeping and drench my couch with tears. My eyes grow weak with sorrow; they fail because of all my foes" (Psalm 6:2–3, 6–7). Or the prophet Habakkuk, crying out to God for justice: "I heard and my heart pounded, my lips quivered at the sound; decay crept into my bones, and my legs trembled" (Habakkuk 3:16).

Suddenly we understand the significance of Hebrews 5:7: "During the days of Jesus' life on earth, he offered up prayers and petitions with fervent cries and tears to the one who could save him from death."

We've never seen Jesus like this before! Sorrowful and troubled? To the point of death? In anguish? Not in a raging storm at sea, not when confronted by a foaming demoniac or a fitful epileptic, not when grilled by religious hypocrites, not in the face of the death of a twelve-year-old girl or the brother of his dear friends. Not even in the face of his own temptation by Satan in the wilderness.

This is new for Jesus. He knew it, and he needed his Father to know it. His life is at stake.[9] If God doesn't intervene, Jesus might die in Gethsemane before he even gets to Golgotha.

Honest prayer unapologetically recognizes human limitations and boldly requests help from the Divine. And honest prayer is heard. Jesus doesn't die in the garden. He dies on the cross, drinking down every dreg of the dreaded cup he had begged to be removed. Ultimately, Jesus' Take This Cup prayer doesn't result in his rescue from the garden but rather in his deliverance through it. The ultimate rescue would be from the death on the cross that follows. Yet still, Jesus prays honest.

Jesus' agonized uncertainty is not a sign of faithlessness or doubt or rebellion against his Father. Rather, his unbridled and honest expression of despair pours out of his humanity. Embattled before the most terrifying ordeal of his earthly existence, Jesus didn't calmly and placidly submit—he brought his whole human being before his heavenly Father. Jesus prayed honest. An honest request in an honest expression: Take this cup. What I want. *My* desire.

Jesus prayed side one of the prayer coin because he was convinced that he would be "safe" to do so. That, in fact, there would be something fulfilling and whole-making and unifying in his request. And God the Father actually desired Jesus' honest pleas, offered with great integrity, as the writer of Hebrews expresses: "and he was heard because of his reverent submission" (Hebrews 5:7).

Honest comes from trust and trust comes from being known. Jesus *knew* that the Father knew his heart, all of it—so Jesus trusted that the Father would hear his raw three-word request.

* * *

*"The prayer preceding all prayers is,
'May it be the real I who speaks.
May it be the real Thou that I speak to.'"*
C. S. LEWIS[10]

• • •

*"How does one continue in prayer
when it seems like all the answers
are no, not now, and wait?"*

LOUISE

CHAPTER 5

Our Honest—
Take This Cup

*". . . take this cup from me;
yet not my will, but yours be done."*
LUKE 22:42

While unpacking a portion of my two weeks' worth of clothes and supplies at the apartment where I was to stay in Australia, I mentally juggled the treatment options that Evan was facing back in Denver. We were scheduled to Facetime again in about ten minutes. I wanted my head clear and my list of questions prepared.

Evan had called me again while I was riding from the airport on the "wrong side" of Terry's car. It seemed everything was on the wrong side just then. The doctors were testing to determine the specific type of blood infection Evan had contracted. Some very scary words were filtering down: streptococcus, staph, MRSA . . . and, perhaps the worst, necrotizing fasciitis. While supporting myself through seminary, I'd worked part-time in an emergency room admissions department. I knew medical terminology. These were not pretty words.

Approaching the empty closet with a wad of clothes in my hands, I went down. To the ground. I wailed. I fetaled. I clawed at the carpet. Jesus-in-the-garden-like, I begged, "Take this cup!" An honest eruption of what I wanted. A tortured plea that God remove what I didn't want.

This posture wasn't completely new to me. But it was rare. I'm not one to lose emotional control—I'd spent most of my childhood and much of my young adulthood hiding much and most of me from everyone, including God. And sometimes even from myself.

Learning to Hide from Honest

From their very beginning, children are honest—innocently honest. "Why is that lady so fat?" "Do all old people have a waggle under their chin like Grandma?" They say what is in their hearts and on their minds, and can't be concocted into anything other than what it is.

Until they learn *not* to be honest.

One day in kindergarten I stealthily observed a classmate offer what seemed a brilliant proclamation just before nap time. Quietly, and likely unnoticed by anyone but me, a little girl approached the teacher and whispered that her tummy hurt. Magically, the teacher swooped down and took her by the hand to the school nurse, returning alone to our classroom just minutes later. After nap time, as I rolled up my doggy-face blanket and returned it to my cubby, I asked my teacher where the girl had gone. "Home," she said. "She had a tummy ache."

Home! I marveled at the power of my classmate's illness. She hadn't looked sick to me. Yet whatever sickness she'd concocted had the power to take her from school to home, just like that!

The next day, as nap time arrived again, I unrolled my doggy mat and lay down obediently. Seconds later, I sprang up, and then, acting my part, dipped my head and approached my teacher. "I have a tummy ache!" I told her.

Sure enough, with compassion equal to the day before, my teacher led me to the school nurse, who popped a thermometer into my mouth. Though no fever registered, my mother was called to come and take me home. It worked! I'd have a free afternoon to do whatever I wanted!

Mother arrived and shuttled me to our waiting white Impala station wagon. When she pulled into the driveway at home, I bounded out of the car and headed toward the backyard swing set. "I'm going to play!" I called over my shoulder.

"Oh, no you're not," came my mother's response. "If you're sick enough to leave school, you're sick enough to go to bed." She ushered me into the house and down the hall to my bedroom, where she closed the blinds and tucked me tightly under my great-grandmother's blue and white quilt. The "sick quilt" we used when someone in the family came down with the flu or something equally awful.

Wait. This wasn't working as I'd planned. I'd thought lying—not being honest—would get me something I wanted. Something I couldn't get any other way.

Yes, as children we are innocently honest . . . until we learn not to be. Sometimes we try on dishonesty, just because we want to test our powers—as I did in kindergarten. Other times we pull away from honesty because we are deeply shamed over our "wrongness," like Adam and Eve hiding from God in the garden of Eden, lying about eating the forbidden fruit (Genesis 3). I can still taste the guilt of pocketing a bright red tube of lipstick from the counter of the local Walgreen's. And the stench of throwing a raw egg through the front door of a neighbor's home while trick-or-treating as a teen. And the "nobody-will-find-out" badness of snatching a pack of my mother's cigarettes and sneaking off to smoke them down at the bayou. On each occasion, I concocted a covering of sorts to disguise my terribleness. When confronted, I went dishonest so I wouldn't be found out.

Sometimes we learn not to be honest because honesty is simply too vulnerable. We've been hurt by honesty, and safety seems to hover through the doorway of hiding—especially hiding the reality of who we are, what we think, and what we do.

I grew up in a home defined by divorce and alcoholism. My father left when I was five years old, and in his wake I bobbed along with barely a nostril above the surface of my childhood swamp of self-condemnation. Surely, if I'd been a better daughter, a more excellent girl, he would have stayed.

In preparation for his annual dinner visits, my mother dressed my older sister and me in petticoated perfection. Then we sat very adult-like at a fancy restaurant table, while sawing at our steaks. We obediently stuffed our napkins into our patent leather belts so as not to lose them to the chair chasms beneath us, and cause our father to growlingly retrieve them.

Returning home to my blearily distracted mother, I'd rock myself to sleep in the belly of my twin bed, sucking my thumb and gnarling my long hair into knots with all-night rotisserie-ing. The next morning, my exasperated mother brushed the tangles out of my hair and into my heart. I would be late for school again. She would be late for work. I was a mess. Real Elisa submerged into a netherworld where I buried my badness and resurfaced with a more pleasing "public" version of myself.

In middle school the strain grew stronger. I assembled the jumbled pieces of my mother's slurred speech, scotchy breath, and inability to get up in the morning (despite her blaring alarm clock) into the recognizable image of alcoholism. I voluntarily assumed the roles of maid, cook, and laundress in a desperate attempt to create an atmosphere of "home," in the hope that my school friends would still like me and accept me if they were to come through the actual front door of my rickety life. Every Saturday, I dumped mounds of cigarette butts into the garbage can, ajaxed the ashtrays, vacuumed our gold pile living room carpet into neat vertical rows, and trailed Lysol aerosol through our ranch-style home in an attempt to quash the stench of the smoke. It wasn't until my post-college days that I learned our furniture wasn't really olive green—it had been "dyed" that hue from years of tobacco absorption.

Even after discovering God's stunning love for me—that he longed so intensely for a relationship with me that he allowed Jesus to die on a cross for my badness—Real Elisa remained beneath the surface. Oh, I'd allow her a shy peep out from behind Public Elisa's legs now and then. A curious stare at the Holy One whose finger had begun to beckon.

As a child, I'd known God was real, a discovery made in the local church where Mother dropped off my sister and me for two and a half hours each Sunday morning. (She was smart, my mother. Free childcare every Sunday and a chance to do errands without us in tow!) Later, my childlike understanding of Jesus morphed into full-out faith when as a teen I learned more about "becoming a Christian" by "asking Jesus into my heart as Savior and Lord." I flung myself into his imagined arms.

But I still kept Real Elisa hidden from his reach.

Until one morning in high school, reading in Romans 8, I came to a section that seared me straight through: "Who shall separate us from the love of Christ? Shall trouble or hardship or persecution or famine or nakedness or danger or sword? . . . No, in all these things we are more than conquerors through him who loved us. For I am convinced that neither death nor life, neither angels nor demons, neither the present nor the future, nor any powers, neither height nor depth, nor anything else in all creation, will be able to separate us from the love of God that is in Christ Jesus our Lord" (Romans 8:35, 37–39).

I paused over each element. Trouble. Hardship. Persecution. Famine. Nakedness. Danger. Sword. For sure, I knew trouble, hardship, and danger. Just living in my home had familiarized me with them. Persecution had arrived with my full-out-faith stage, as several family members considered me more than overzealous. Famine—I was always hungry. Sword? Did spankings count? Or other pains that accompanied my growing up, like a broken arm while running in the sprinkler or a concussion suffered after a horseback-ride fall?

Wait. *Nakedness.*

The thought hit me in the shower—amidst my vulnerable exposure, there in our shamefully decaying bathroom with the green-grey tiles slowly detaching from the wall. Where I squinted through half-closed eyes in the middle of the night, not wanting to catch a glimpse of the cockroaches scurrying back down the bathtub drain when the light flicked on.

Even there, nothing could separate me from the love of God in Christ Jesus.

Later I read in Hebrews 4:13, "Nothing in all creation is hidden from God's sight. Everything is uncovered and laid bare before the eyes of him to whom we must give account."

Oh my.

With the skill of a deep-sea diver on a rescue mission, God began his descent to find me. Real Elisa. To bring me back to the surface where light, oxygen and love would meet my need. Really, it's been an ongoing rescue mission, as over the years God has continued to bring more and more areas of me up from hiding into the healing of his presence.

Re-Learning Honest

I'm wondering . . . what's the most honest prayer I've ever prayed?

Heal my mother of alcoholism. Bring my father to believe in you. As I found my voice with God, my earliest prayers were Take This Cup prayers. Take this brokenness and make my family whole. Give me what I want. Remove what I don't want.

When, despite my prayers, my family's brokenness continued, I determined to craft a perfectly intact *second* family. I met and married Evan, stable rock of a man, and we pledged we would never even use the word *divorce*. Knowing we could not have children biologically, we adopted two babies and raised them with joy and a deep commitment to marriage and to Jesus. A passion we prayed they would one day share.

Deep into their teen years—with me in my long-term tenure as CEO of MOPS International, a nonprofit ministry focused on meeting new moms in their need for Jesus—our children steered off my ideal path of perfection and into ruts that included teen pregnancy, addiction, and struggle after struggle.

I know Take This Cup prayers. "Take this cup!" I've prayed over my children's choices. "Take this cup!" I've prayed over the broken me I discovered as a result of my responses to their choices. "Take this cup!" I've prayed as a nonprofit leader facing the challenge of accomplishing a vital mission with too few resources. "Take this cup!" I've prayed as a dear friend was diagnosed with Stage 4 cancer. "Take this cup!" I've prayed in my marriage, in my mothering, in my career, in my neighborhood, and in my extended family relationships. Take this cup!

And yet, as I consider Jesus' version of honest, I'm challenged as to how honest I've really been with God. Is there more honesty than what I've discovered so far? What if I made Jesus' honest prayer Real Elisa's honest prayer?

It's a powerful thought to consider, that Jesus' honest Take This Cup prayer can be the model for our own prayerful exchanges with our Father.

Okay, there's *no way* we are asked to take the cup that Jesus took: the ultimate cup of punishment. So there's no way we should ask to be released from it, right?

Right.

Also, because Jesus drank the cup of suffering—all of it—any "cup" we hold has already had the sting of eternal consequences removed.

True again.

But there's something else Take This Cup prayer offers for us, for you and me. Because Jesus was completely honest—agonizingly honest in asking God to remove the cup, yet ready to drink the cup as God directed—we can be honest too in asking God to remove the cup of our daily deaths. Tim Keller puts it this way: "Jesus' prayers were given the rejection that we sinners merit so that our prayers could have the reception that he merits."[1]

Take This Cup prayer is "what I want" prayer. A plea to remove the pains and sacrifices we face in our lives. This grief. This rejection. This misunderstanding. This injustice. This addiction. This debt. This loneliness. This not-enoughness. This shame.

Take This Cup prayer also might mean, "Give me what I don't have in my life that I want." Jesus prayed "take this cup" as in "remove it"—and he also prayed, "but if that isn't possible, give me what I need to drink it." Take this singleness when I want to be married, or give me joy in my singleness. Take this dead-end job when I want more meaningful employment, or give me peace in this current role. Take this impasse with my teen when I want a closer relationship, or give me uncondi-tional love for my child.

We pause and ponder how we could follow Jesus' example and pray our own version of "Take this cup." *Gasp*—isn't that selfish? How does our pain compare to what Jesus endured?

It doesn't. Of course it doesn't. But our pain is still our pain. Jesus prayed his prayer coin of honest and abandon, embracing the intimacy he possessed with the Father and modeling the intimacy we too can possess. If he died to provide such a relationship, how can we *not* enter in ourselves?

In fact, by not praying our own version of "take this cup," we might actually be doubting God. As if he isn't able. As if he isn't God enough to act in the matters that concern us.

Let's Be Honest

Wait, how honest are we talking? Jesus prayed an honestly human request in an honestly human expression. Jesus *experienced* the pain. That honest?

What if we pray in deep distress, overwhelmed with sorrow, risking the vulnerability of wailing out to God our deepest longings and needs and wants and desires to the point that *we* experience our utter humanness before him? The pain. The struggle in all its reality. About our kids, our money concerns, our marriages, our health, our jobs, our nation, our churches, our addictions, our woundings?

Immediately, holes are poked in our defenses, and objections fly out of us. If we pour our hearts out to God in this way . . . then what? Will he listen? Will he get mad? Will he zap us with even worse circumstances? Will he answer? Will it make any difference?

After a lifetime of waiting for love, C. S. Lewis lost his precious wife, Joy, just four years into marriage. Cataloging his pain in *A Grief Observed*, he writes, "What chokes every prayer and every hope is the memory of all the prayers [Joy] and I offered and all the false hopes we had. Not hopes raised merely by our own wishful thinking, hopes encouraged, even forced upon us, by false diagnoses, by X-ray photographs, by strange remissions, by one temporary recovery that might have ranked as a miracle. Step by step we were 'led up the garden path.' Time after time, when He seemed most gracious He was really preparing the next torture."[2]

That's pretty honest.

Applying this straight talk to prayer, Lewis writes, "We must lay before Him what is in us, not what ought to be in us."[3]

Honest honest.

Since I began this book—not my prayer coin journal but the writing of this manuscript—my neck has flamed with pain. I imagine the source: too many granted "uppies" for my two-year-old grandson, Dominic; helping my brother move furniture, flower pots, and boxes in his new home; lugging my luggage across London from airport to train to tube stop for a speaking engagement. I sit to write with a bowed heart and my neck screams objections.

Honestly, God, take this cup of pain. This cup of interference. This cup of what I don't want.

I imagine this "cup" as a balloon goblet of red wine, poured out in a lavish gesture of celebration, its aroma inviting me to raise its merriment to my lips. That's what the process of writing a book should be like, right? A joy! An act of creation! An elegant effort, from a desk heaped with tablets of inspiring notes and pithy discoveries.

I raise the goblet to my mouth, tasting its contents on my tongue and—it stings. Bitter. A vinegar shock.

Reflexively, I spew it out. The liquid rains horizontal, splattering down on my white shirt. A spray of burgundy stains my world.

What seemed bright with hope as I settled in at my computer now sours. I wince with the pain in my neck. I do not want to write this book. I do not want to drink this cup. Take it.

In her book *Present over Perfect*, Shauna Niequist tells of a friend who compared prayer to oil and vinegar, which are both needed. The acidic vinegar of life struggles rests on top of the rich and flavorful oil. "Many of us learned along the way to ignore the vinegar—the hot tears banging on our eyelids, the hurt feelings, the fear. Ignore them. Stuff them. Make yourself numb. And then pray dutiful, happy prayers. But this is what I'm learning about prayer: you don't get the oil until you pour out the vinegar."[4]

Move the vinegar. Make way for the oil. I consider going all-out honest in my prayer coin efforts, as Max Lucado directs: "*Pray your pain out*. Pound the table. March up and down the lawn. . . . Angry at God? Disappointed with his strategy? Ticked off at his choices? Let him know it."[5]

Can he—God—handle my pounding prayers? I want to think he can. I retrace Jesus' honest and begin to believe that, surely, God can. Because he heard and responded to the puckered prayers of his Son.

I scrawl Take This Cup across a fresh left page in my prayer coin journal. I stare at the words, reflecting on the dismay I feel over my neck and the resulting clog in my writing. Is there something this knotted seize can teach me? A tangle in my neck teasing out into a tangle in my spirit? A clustered clump that halts me to consider just what it is I'm learning about honest?

I shift position. And I realize I'm worrying over words and doubting my own worthiness on this topic of prayer. The grip tightens, like a Vulcan hand "Spocking" my shoulder with a nerve pinch just below the neck. While I don't quite splay to the floor in unconsciousness, I'm still knocked off balance. I'm not a fancy Bible scholar. Yes, I went to seminary a million years ago. Yes, I unfold God's Word in daily discovery with my radio teammates. Yes, I've sensed the Holy Spirit whisper surprising thoughts about passages as I read. But this prayer dare? Who do I think I am?

Take this cup! I'm not enough! I don't even know the books of the Bible in order! (Did you know there is a table of contents at the beginning of every single edition of Scripture? What a relief!)

"Take this cup" is soooooooo—what?—human? Needy? Revealing? Inappropriate?

Maybe I'll skip this side. . . .

In my best being, I know that something is missed when I avoid honesty. Something raw and scary, yes, but something essential to living. When I cover up my needs with defensive self-protection, I shield myself not just from the world's wounding but also from heaven's wooing. Honest can be our teacher, if we allow it to do its work.

I want acceptance: the kind of tolerant presence that receives whatever is, or isn't in me. I want love: unconditional, never-turn-your-back, no-matter-what-love.

Even more, I want freedom: the very honest admission of what I *don't* want, like neck problems.

So again, I turn my attention back to my journal and my current Take This Cup. What is the issue? For sure distraction . . . and of course, pain . . . but I sense something else. I realize I'm afraid. Of more than the ever-present not-enoughness. I'm also afraid of the lurking presence of an evil one who doesn't want me to pray this way, much less write about it. A sneaky thief slithering through my thinking, reaching out to steal my joy of contribution. *You don't know what you're talking about!* he hisses. *Shut up and go vacuum. Or go to the store. Or zone out in front of the TV. No? Well, take this!* And another zing shoots through my shoulder.

Staying honest, I ask God to remove the pain yet again. Take this cup! And then comes a realization, right there in the honest. Something I hadn't seen, hadn't felt. Perhaps something I haven't *wanted* to see or feel. Take this pain *that signals my need*.

Need. I need you, God. I can't do this on my own. Help. Me.

What if you sensed the pain not as pain but as my presence with you in the writing? What if each time you feel the pain, you understand that it is I, laying my hand on your being, reminding you that I know your need and am present to meet it? And what if I'm trying to show you that you don't have to do this work alone but that I long to do it with you?

But I don't want you that close, God. I like being in control and believing I can do life on my own.

Bam!

Take This Cup is revealing. Honest prayer searches the dark crevices in my cranium, ejecting the truth and laying it open for dissection. For examination. So I can see what it is I really want or don't want. So I can own it and decide.

Dare I go this honest? Before God? (And before the rest of the world reading these words in print?) Margaret Feinberg woos me with her words, "Prayer is the place where I'm invited to present the parts of myself that no one else sees to a God who already knows and loves me anyway."[6]

I remember Hebrews 4:13, and then read beyond it:

Nothing in all creation is hidden from God's sight. Everything is uncovered and laid bare before the eyes of him to whom we must give account.

Therefore, since we have a great high priest who has ascended into heaven, Jesus the Son of God, let us hold firmly to the faith we profess. For we do not have a high priest who is unable to empathize with our weaknesses, but we have one who has been tempted in every way, just as we are—yet he did not sin. Let us then approach God's throne of grace with confidence, so that we may receive mercy and find grace to help us in our time of need. (Hebrews 4:13–16)

Jesus prayed honest before his Father because he knew he could. And then Jesus died that we might access honest prayer before our Father too.

How honest? All the way back, to Real Elisa. To childhood honesty honest.

Barriers to Honest

Let's keep at this a bit more. Why do I still hold back? (Why do you?) Do I somehow believe I'm the "exception" to God's love? That he is capable of loving everyone, everywhere, *except* me? I'm too bad. Too selfish. Too unfiltered. Too ungodly. Too un-everything.

I picture him knowing my twisted thoughts and, in my mind, he turns away, shrugging at my resistance, shaking his head in disgust.

Silly Elisa.

Sherry Harney nudges me, "Stop and think about what we are saying when we lock up our frustration and swallow our sorrow. We are acting like God can't handle our honest expressions of pain and anger. We are pretending that God does not know."[7]

The psalmist knew better.

> You have searched me, Lord,
> and you know me.
> You know when I sit and when I rise;
> you perceive my thoughts from afar.
> You discern my going out and my lying down;
> you are familiar with all my ways.
> Before a word is on my tongue
> you, Lord, know it completely.
> You hem me in behind and before,
> and you lay your hand upon me.

Such knowledge is too wonderful for me,
    too lofty for me to attain.
Where can I go from your Spirit?
    Where can I flee from your presence?
If I go up to the heavens, you are there;
    if I make my bed in the depths, you are
    there.
If I rise on the wings of the dawn,
    if I settle on the far side of the sea,
even there your hand will guide me,
    your right hand will hold me fast.
If I say, "Surely the darkness will hide me
    and the light become night around me,"
even the darkness will not be dark to you;
    the night will shine like the day,
    for darkness is as light to you.
                    (Psalm 139:1–12)

Reality is that even in my honest, ugly-to-me Take This Cup moments, God sees me—and still loves me. And then he does even more! He goes so far as to figure out how to express my "honest" for me when I have no words. He looks into my being, gathering my needs and folding them into utterances that have his attention, even though I may not be able to fully understand them. "If we don't know how or what to pray, it doesn't matter. He does our praying in and for us, making prayer out of our wordless sighs, our aching groans. He knows us far better than we know ourselves, knows our pregnant condition, and keeps us present before God. That's why we can be so sure that every detail in our lives of love for God is worked into something good" (Romans 8:27–28 MSG).

Honest Changes Us

So I bring "me." Honest me. Real Elisa. And you know what happens? In the honest, in the Take This Cup, before I even get to the tip of abandon in Not My Will, I learn. I grow. I receive. Because there is something that happens in my honest that opens me to understand and know a part of me and a part of God that I couldn't access before. So now I can be even more honest. Perhaps honest enough to understand what I really need— help to simply let God help me.

I'm not the only one to stumble upon such a discovery. Anne Lamott brings a modern spin, "Sometimes the first time we pray, we cry out in the deepest desperation, 'God help me.' This is a great prayer, as we are then at our absolutely most degraded and isolated, which means we are nice and juicy with the consequences of our best thinking and possibly teachable."[8] Don't you love that? Nice and juicy . . . and possibly teachable.

Honest opens us to help. And help that wholly heals comes from God alone. Take This Cup prayer is honest prayer that brings all of us to all of God. What we want. What we don't want. What we've done. What we haven't done. What we need. What we don't need. Our mistakes and wanderings. Our dreamiest desires. Our longings and leanings. Our selfish musings and our selfless yearnings.

Honest changes us and honest changes the way we pray. Like the gradual unwrapping of a bandaged wound, honest reveals what is hurt and what can be made whole. When we are revealed, we can be healed.

Bottom line: honest prayer has the power to make us better. In opening honest, we open up to change. We see more of what we really want and therefore who we really are. We peer into the depths of the cup God has allowed in our days—the one we thrust back at him—and he helps us to see what is truly there: a certain "shame shroud" that keeps us in a corner, clinging to our own way and therefore running from God's aid. Philip Yancey admits, "Self-exposure is never easy, but when I do it I learn that underneath the layers of grime lies a damaged work of art that God longs to repair."[9] A repair made possible only because of Jesus' prayer coin preparation and his ultimate obedience on the cross.

Where Honest Takes Us

How sensible, yet surprising, it is to recognize that the way out of the shame shroud that shields us from honest is actually vulnerability.

Really?

Researcher and storyteller Brene Brown shatters our preconceptions about vulnerability.[10] We don't really choose or not choose to be vulnerable so we can't really protect ourselves from the potential of vulnerability. As humans, we *are* vulnerable: open to hurt. Such a condition is not a result of the Fall but rather, one manufactured in our creation. And as we were modeled after God, made in his image, it stands to reason that our experience of vulnerability is also his. God is vulnerable.[11]

Think about it. In offering humankind free will, God opened himself to wounding and rejection as well as to love. When we went running from him in the first garden, appalled at our sinfulness to the point of hiding from our very Source, he came looking for us, seeking ongoing connection.[12]

God not only knows us and still loves us, he *wants* us. All of us. He offers us the connection he enjoys in the Trinity. An unbreakable intimacy that flows from love.

When our first grandson was just a small child, he and his then-single mother lived with my husband and me. That season of life was bursting with busy and, while challenging, was lavishly ladled with God's love.

One evening my husband told little Marcus that he would be gone several days on a business trip. Marcus loved his BeePeez dearly, and his eyes widened at the thought of the upcoming separation.

He gulped his breath and squeezed words out of a heavy heart: "But BeePeez, when you come back will you *find* me?"

"Of course, Bubby," my husband replied. "I will *always* find you."

God is like that with us. The ultimately vulnerable One will hunt for us and find us in our pretense of defense. While he sees straight through to the real us, he will wait until we unmask our most covered-up pleas. He will give us his ear as we peel back layer after layer of what we want and what we don't want until we understand our need for the help only he can give.

The psalmist confidently mirrors the need for the help only God can give: "Because he bends down to listen, I will pray as long as I have breath!" (Psalm 116:2 NLT)

What's in your cup that you want God to take? Your less-than-satisfying marriage? Your untreatable disease? Your child's choices that defy your guidance? Your frustrating job? Your unending loneliness? Your suffocating grief?

Take this cup. I lean in to the honest of my Take This Cup desires and what they are teaching me. Honest shows me I need God. He isn't asking me to write a book about prayer without praying.

Side one of our two-sided prayer coin begins honest. The deep dive necessary to discover what we can ultimately enjoy in the presence of God through prayer starts off with Take This Cup. What I want. What I don't want. What you want. What you don't want. When we start honest—with ourselves and with God—we ready ourselves to receive not just what we think we want but what our good God wants for us.

Honest.

• • •

"When our prayers lack honesty,
they lack power."
SHERRY HARNEY[13]

• • •

"There's always this thing in the back of my head that somehow I will experience negative or bad results because I allowed myself to be vulnerable before the Lord. Because of the 'chicken' in me, I am going to start with something I consider easy to do. And I'm going to increasingly add bigger things as I go into the challenge. There. I said it. I just opened myself up to be very vulnerable before God."

CHERYL

CHAPTER 6

Jesus' Abandon—
Not My Will

"... take this cup from me;
*yet **not my will, but yours be done.**"*
LUKE 22:42

Jesus prayed honest, "Take this cup." But now, in the same breath, in the same sentence, he prays another prayer, seemingly the opposite of the one he just spoke. Side two of Jesus' prayer coin.

Three other words express perhaps the most chilling moment of relinquishment ever endured: Not my will.

Translated: Not what I want.

Mark records Jesus' words as, "not what I will, but what you will" (Mark 14:36). In *The Message*, Eugene Peterson paraphrases, "Papa, Father, you can—can't you?—get me out of this. Take this cup away from me. But please, not what I want—what do *you* want?"

I yield what I want. What do you want, Father?

A prayer of abandon.

I struggle to describe Jesus' yielding. As if selecting a pair of shoes for a lengthy sightseeing trip over cobbled roads, muddy paths, and tiled floors—what will work best, not give me blisters, protect my feet?—I slip various words over the concept to discern their "fit."

Surrender: Give in. Admit defeat. Relinquish.

No . . . too militaristic. Win/lose.

Submit: Give over. Give up. Sit under.

So much about power and powerlessness. No. . . .

Relinquish: Give up. Synonyms: *hand over, renounce, resign, bow out.*

Better. But some emotion rises up that I have trouble naming. Or are these words just not my style?

Abandon: To give up completely. To give up with the intent of never claiming a right or interest in. To give oneself over without restraint.[1]

Wow. That's pretty non-negotiable . . . yet compelling. Yes. Abandon. Yielding my way—and doing so without condition. Abandoned in request and in emotion. Abandoned abandon. That strikes me as powerful.

Not my will. Not what I want. But what you will. What do *you* want, God? Or again, in Peterson's words, "Do it your way" (Matthew 26:42 MSG).

Just a few chapters back, we faced our stunned surprise as Jesus dared to go honest in side one of his prayer coin: Take This Cup. His bold request. His unhinged expression. Jesus turned *honest* and laid bare the "what I want" side of his prayer coin. Unapologetically human, Jesus asked honest. Take this cup.

Turning over from the honest side of his prayer coin, Jesus now says, "Not *my* will"—and we feel the impression of honest still with him. Our fingers trace his heart's yearning that God take this cup, even while he offers a stuttering "N–n–not *my* will." It's as if he recognizes his still divergent desire in the moment *because* he has just honestly prayed "take this cup." Mirrored in his two-sided garden prayer, Jesus' honest reflects back to him— and he measures a gap between human and divine.

Abandon Comes from Choice

Unless we pause with Jesus in this moment, we might miss the point altogether. We expect Jesus in this place, engaging the autopilot of abandon to the divine. After all, his God-ness would of course teeter him over to this side, right?

We're actually a bit surprised that there is any gap, Jesus being God and all. It's been new information to consider a Jesus torn in this way. But we do pause, because the honest Take This Cup side of Jesus has created disequilibrium in our beings. We're eager to tip him back over into the "Good Jesus" abandon. But what we've just come to learn about him has made Jesus even more dear to us—more raw, more real—and therefore more essential and connected. We want *all* of Jesus. The honest *and* the abandon.

Take this cup. Honest. We dip ourselves into this territory, trusting God will hear and handle and that he will somehow use honest to make us better. Like children who imprint off the pattern of parents, we consider mimicking our Savior's honest posture.

Take this cup. What I want. We linger with Jesus there.

Then it happens: the flip. Jesus turns abandon. Not my will. What *God* wants. A committed yielding of his very personal need. A solid relinquishment of Jesus' choice in favor of the choice of the Father. An alignment of his destiny with the divine desire.

For Jesus, abandon wasn't a blind leap of faith or a lobotomized submission. True submission can never be forced or demanded. Oh, I suppose the relinquishment that comes from being conquered can be actualized as one adapts to it. But that kind of surrender comes with a superior control in which the will of one entity reigns over another's. The Father never asked that of Jesus. This kind of abandon—Jesus' abandoned abandon—can only be offered voluntarily.

Ponder the mind-set of Jesus from Philippians 2. Jesus, "who, being in very nature God, did not consider equality with God something to be used to his own advantage; rather, he made himself nothing by taking the very nature of a servant, being made in human likeness. And being found in appearance as a man, he humbled himself by becoming obedient to death—even death on a cross!" (verses 6–8).

Consider each element:

- Jesus didn't consider equality with God something to be used to his advantage.
- Jesus made himself nothing.
- Jesus took the very nature of a servant.
- Jesus humbled himself by becoming obedient to death.

These were Jesus' voluntary actions. God the Father did not force them upon the Son. Jesus underlines this idea in John 10:18: "No one takes [my life] from me, but I lay it down of my own accord."

Abandon, then, comes from choice. But be clear, Jesus' lifestyle of abandon didn't prevent him from struggling. As we've seen, Jesus was unendingly riddled as a human, longing for the reunion of his divine being when his assignment on earth was complete.

On those lonely nights on this planet, after days of work exorcising and healing and restoring—then enduring insults and arrogance and stubborn rebellion—how Jesus must have longed to return to the Father's side! And when he met Elijah and Moses atop a mountain, experiencing a transfiguration of his being before Peter, James, and John, didn't Jesus yearn to return to his Father's presence with those Old Testament heroes rather than trudge down the mountain with his beloved but befuddled companions?

Jesus was tempted, *really* tempted, to choose his will over that of the Father. But in his temptation, Jesus chose abandon. "He did not sin," as Hebrews 4:15 says. Or, as the apostle Paul writes, "Christ did not please himself" (Romans 15:3).

Abandon Comes from Love

Such a sacrificial choice to abandon comes from love. Jesus' abandon wasn't a matter of God compelling his Son, forcing his will on him, but rather of the Son willingly and intimately embracing and embodying his Abba's self-giving love.[2]

Jesus' abandon in the garden, side two of his prayer coin, expresses the abandon of love he exhibited throughout his life on earth, the ongoing denial and relinquishment of his will for the will of the Father.

Jesus wrestled mightily with the enemy *while* surrendering his will to the Father's. As he told his disciples, "the prince of this world is coming. He has no hold over me, but he comes so that the world may learn that I love the Father and do exactly what my Father has commanded me" (John 14:30–31).

Reread that. Jesus *loves* the Father and does *exactly* what the Father commands him. Even when his human will differs. *Take this cup!* Even when deserted by his closest friends. *Then he returned to his disciples and found them sleeping.* Even when troubled in his soul to the point of death. *My soul is overwhelmed to the point of death.* Even when agonized in body so that small blood vessels burst, mingling with the cursed sweat . . . *and his sweat was like drops of blood falling to the ground.*

Jesus chose abandon, and he chose it out of love.

John is the only gospel writer who doesn't specifically mention the prayer coin. Instead, he simply displays Jesus' ultimate alignment after he's tossed the coin in the air in a repetitive prayer of anguish. In the fourth Gospel, Jesus solidly stands on his ground of choice. When Peter draws a sword to defend Jesus from the pursuing soldiers, lopping off the ear of the high priest's servant Malchus, Jesus responds, "Shall I not drink the cup the

Father has given me?" (John 18:11). Not my will. Not what I want, but what God wants.

In the garden, Jesus turned to the second side of his prayer coin out of a careful understanding—a remembering of what he knew to be true about the Father and his relationship with him. We can trace Jesus' logic through Scripture:

- The Son was one with the Father. "In the beginning was the Word, and the Word was with God, and the Word was God" (John 1:1).

- The Son trusted the Father. Jesus laid down his godly attributes to walk this world as a human being, but he never laid down his relationship with the Father (see Philippians 2:5–8).

- The Son knew that the Father loved him, and Jesus loved him back through obedience (Matthew 3:17; Mark 1:11; Luke 3:22).

- The Son shared the mind of the Father and knew that he came to earth to save the world (John 3:16, 12:27).

- The Son knew the Father had given him all authority—so he had a choice (John 13:3).

- The Son loved the Father and wanted to please him in all things (John 17:4, 26).

Utter abandon is an exorbitant action, and one that was necessary for the work of the cross to be completed. Jesus knew he would unjustly be seen as sin, when he was not sinful at all (2 Corinthians 5:21). But he submitted his desire to the will of the Father, knowing that God would accomplish good for him and for all. Jesus prayed a prayer of absolute abandon because he knew the Father trusted and loved him, and he trusted and loved the Father back.

Even after praying the prayer coin, as Jesus rose to face his betrayer, the guards, the religious and Roman authorities, and the crowds, he continued choosing abandon: "For the joy set before him he endured the cross, scorning its shame, and sat down at the right hand of the throne of God" (Hebrews 12:2).

The writer of Hebrews summarized Jesus' experience like this: "Son though he was, he learned obedience from what he suffered" (Hebrews 5:8).

Abandon Grows from Obedience

Jesus learned? Obedience? Through what he suffered? How did that happen?

I'm intrigued by Luke's mention of an angel attending to Jesus at Gethsemane (Luke 22:43). Angels were not new to Jesus; of course, he knew of them helping humans throughout history. On his journey to Mount Horeb, Elijah was helped by an angel (1 Kings 19:5–8). An angel appeared to Daniel and provided a sustaining vision (Daniel 10:1–19). Angels appeared to Mary and Joseph, Jesus' earthly parents (Luke 1:26; Matthew 1:20). And angels presented themselves to Jesus, himself—in the desert wilderness, at the end of his forty-day-and-night temptation and battle with his Enemy, "the devil left him, and angels came and attended him" (Matthew 4:11). Angels would also appear at his empty tomb (John 20:12).

But here, in the garden, the angel comes as a demonstration, a medium, of God's presence and provision, just as Jesus is facing the ultimate separation from his Father.[3] In agony, stressed to the point that his body was failing, Jesus offers his two-sided prayer: "take this cup from me; yet not my will, but yours be done" (Luke 22:42). And then, in the very next verse, "An angel from heaven appeared to him and strengthened him" (Luke 22:43).

The Greek word translated *strengthened* here is the same one used to describe the apostle Paul, who "regained his strength" after fasting three days following his encounter with the risen Christ (Acts 9:19). Jesus received a physical empowering to endure what would come next.

What would come next would be a chosen—but necessary—abandon. Jesus' choice of abandon, relinquishing himself completely to God's desires, would result in his own abandonment by his Father. "My God, my God, why have you forsaken me?" he cried (Matthew 27:46; Mark 15:34). Jesus' abandon resulted in God's abandonment of him—so that you and I would never be abandoned. As Tim Keller puts it, "Jesus was forgotten so that we could be remembered."[4]

I see a cumulative process in the work of prayer. R. C. Sproul comments, "Prayer prompts and nurtures obedience, putting the heart into proper 'frame of mind' to desire obedience."[5] Prayer creates honesty which develops trust and results in surrender. What a powerful process! Prayer creates honesty. Honesty develops trust. Trust results in surrender. Head over heels, we fall, surrendered, into love.

This two-sided prayer shapes us. It teaches us. It changes us. Perhaps this was the point of the biblical writer who indicated that Jesus went to school with his prayer coin as "he learned obedience from what he suffered" (Hebrews 5:8).

No one would or could drink the cup of suffering apart from the sovereign design and omnipotent strength flowing from divine love. Jesus' motivation was love responding to Love. As Jesus uttered his two-sided prayer of honest abandon, God provided what he needed to choose the outcome—the strengthening presence of an angel helped Jesus follow the path of obedience and die on the cross for us. Abandon is a choice, coming from love that grows from obedience.

Jesus tossed the prayer coin up in the air, honest first, then flipping to abandon. The coin spun between the two, as Jesus' desires met the Father's will, until they settled to the ground in union.

Thy will be done. On earth as it is in heaven.

. . .

*"The Spirit teaches me to yield my will entirely
to the will of the Father. . . . He opens my ear
to wait in great gentleness and teachableness
of soul for what the Father day by day has to
speak and to teach. He shows me how union
with God's will (and the love of it) is union
with God Himself. Entire surrender to God's
will is the Father's claim, the Son's example,
and the true blessedness of the soul."*

ANDREW MURRAY[6]

. . .

*"'Not my will' is a really tough prayer to pray.
I come to God asking for things to go my
way—my will. To resolve that as God's child,
Christ's disciple, his will is best for me is a long
journey of building trust in the relationship.
I wonder if his will is truly best for me or best
for the world. I want it to be best for me,
but if Jesus had wanted what was best for him,
the world would not have been saved."*

ERIN

CHAPTER 7

Our Abandon—
Not My Will

". . . take this cup from me;
*yet **not my will, but yours be done**."*
Luke 22:42

During my initial panic in Australia, some nine thousand miles away from my husband in a Denver ICU, I heard God's whisper of perspective, *"This is about the kids, Elisa."* In the first hours, these words helped. I leaned heavily into them, tasking both my son and my daughter with certain "to-do's" for their father. After all, there was nothing else I could do.

Not my will. Abandon.

But just as I tilted to this side two of the prayer coin, new honest pleas weighted it away from abandon and back in the direction of honest.

FEBRUARY 24 [EVENING]
Take This Cup

- *I'm "stuck" in Melbourne for the moment and so am committed to the first conference tomorrow morning. But should I go home immediately after? I could be in Denver for three days and then return across the Pacific for the second conference the next weekend. Could I survive that? Is that enough time to be with Evan? Enough time to be in Australia? Take this cup! Show me how I can get home—or heal Evan so that it's okay for me to be here.*

And with the new honest came the call to a new abandon.

Not My Will

- *I know in my heart that you want to use this development for our good and your glory. I can see it will grow our kids in understanding their need for you and our need for them. In just a few hours, you've already shown me the powerful network of Evan's work life through his staff here, as well as our support from friends who are responding to my prayer texts. Neither of us is alone, even though we are not together. Not my will. What do you want, God?*

Approaching Abandon

Recall how we've defined *abandon*. To give up completely. To give up with the intent of never again claiming a right or interest in. To give oneself over without restraint.

What if we prayed this way? Not my will. Not my desire for my husband to be healthy . . . for my teenager to return home . . . for my parents to ask for help in their elderly years . . . for my boss to keep me employed despite budget cuts . . . for my friend to apologize for her careless words. Not my will.

What then? There's a kind of relinquishment here that we may not be comfortable with. A giving over of what I long for, what I believe is right and best and good to what God somehow sees—something that is beyond me and my understanding. A giving up of what I want for what God wants.

Dare we pray this way? Not my will? Might simply speaking these words somehow prepare us, teach us, even enable us to pray a sincere prayer of abandon?

To be honest—yes, still—it seems to me that we followers of Christ need to be careful here. We can too easily default to what I call an "auto-abandon." As if we're supposed to surrender, so we do. Thy will be done. There—settled, done. But in our heart of hearts, beneath our outward confession of relinquishment, we're like toddlers holding tightly to a stuffed toy, a blankie, a pacifier of what we truly believe will provide the comfort and protection we've come to depend on. Often, in that innermost spot, it's not God.

Auto-abandon isn't really abandon. It something more like resignation.

Avoiding Abandon

What holds us back from true abandon? I don't have to dig far for an answer. My reasons echo my reasons for hiding from honesty. Abandon isn't safe. Hissy lies slither beneath the surface of my days and nights, coiling their untruths through my thinking.

And I listen as they say, *God will hurt me. Surely, he can't love someone like me. Maybe God isn't even good.*

I return to my prayer journal, once again concerned over Evan's health. But I pause to consider other items on the horizon, scrawling a new entry under Take This Cup:

> *Oh, God, take this cup of a family member who is unemployed. I'm sooooo worried about how they will pay their bills! What will unemployment do to their marriage?*

Honest flows. And then, obediently, I shift my attention to the right side of my journal: Not My Will.

Before I even begin to write, a thought erupts. *Yikes! You're not going to suggest that they come live with us? Are you?* And there's the first of the lies: *God is going to hurt you.*

I teeter on the precipice of abandon. My hand hesitates. Not. My. Will. I stutter the offer to God, not really meaning any of the three syllables.

No way can they come live with us! I'll get all enmeshed in their choices. I'll lose myself. I'll lose my relationship with my husband. My dogs will go nuts with their dogs sharing our space.

Not *your* will. Mine instead.

I lift my pen, stepping back from the edge of abandon and returning to the safety of honest, wiping my brow and *phewing* in relief.

I try again. Surely I can turn to abandon. . . .

Rereading my honest Take This Cup entry, I hope to ramp up to abandon, finding enough momentum to jump the divide. *Seriously God, give this person a job! But let's not go to the them-living-with-us-scenario, okay? What are you trying to do to me? We don't make enough to support two families!* Take this cup!

Then the second lie whispers, *God can't possibly love this wormy, selfish part of me.*

I return to all that I'm learning about Jesus' honest and how it applies to my honest. I'm slowly believing that God hears honest. But instead of launching me to abandon, my honest seems to hold me in place like a weight around my feet. I stiffen. *Not your will.* I still want mine.

Mark Batterson, author of the best-selling book on prayer *The Circle Maker*, challenges my thinking. "God is not a genie in a bottle, and your wish is not His command," he writes. "His command better be your wish. . . . And until His sovereign will becomes your sanctified wish, your prayer life will be unplugged from its power supply."[1]

Oh dear. His sovereign will? That's intimidating. And powerful. I squint across the chasm between honest and abandon and consider yet another attempt.

Then it comes, forming in the fog of ambivalence. Yet another reason I fear, perhaps the core cause—a wacky thought really, but it comes: *God is not good.* Lie number three.

I consider a pronouncement often attributed to

Oswald Chambers, "The root of all sin is the suspicion that God is not good." I sigh. Back to the left. *God, take this cup of unemployment. Please, please, please provide a job? So that my dear ones don't suffer any more? And me either?*

I realign, literally picking up my writing hand with my other, as if it's become paralyzed and needs an assist. I place my hand, pen tip down, on the right: Not My Will.

Okay, Lord, I know you have your eye on the end-game of life: eternity. You can use everything. But hon-estly (yes, I flip back here), *maybe you care* too *much about spiritual formation. Of my loved ones. Of me. I don't want to be formed or shaped or changed. I want the security of knowing that a paycheck will be depos-ited each month, so that mouths will be fed and bills will be paid and savings will be accumulated.*

Even though I'm truly right-handed, my stubborn digits will not stay on the right side, will not form the words. I keep sliding left.

Not your will. I want mine.

Apparently, I'm not alone in this feeling. C. S. Lewis, in his book *A Grief Observed*, tells us that God can never be used as simply a way to get things. "If you're approaching Him not as the goal but as a road, not as the end but as a means," he writes, "you're not really approaching Him at all."[2]

Uh-oh.

Honestly, honest is freeing and forming. Honest prayer makes us better because it drags out the real and presents it freely before the One who can truly free us. Honest is great, essential even. But when I pray *only* honest, Take This Cup—what I want—I don't ever allow for what *God* wants. Or when I pray auto-abandon, without the genuine yielding of risk, I never touch the truth of honest where the ultimate freeing works. I may as well not even have God in my life. I think I'm better at Godding than he is.

Richard Foster describes the situation well:

> As we are learning to pray we discover an interesting progression. In the beginning our will is in struggle with God's will. We beg. We pout. We demand. We expect God to perform like a magician or shower us with blessings like Father Christmas. We major in instant solutions and manipulative prayers.
>
> As difficult as this time of struggle is, we must never despise it or try to avoid it. It is an essential part of our growing and deepening in things spiritual.[3]

Maybe honest can nudge me into abandon? One baby step of honest, prodding me into one baby step of abandon, while listening to what God is saying in each? Watching for what he wants to show me?

Baby Steps to Abandon— Answers to Our Avoidance

Let's go back to Jesus. How he did honest. How he got to abandon.

Oh, but he's *Jesus*, you say. I know. That's the point.

We need to let Jesus stomp on the lies that wriggle through our thinking here.

Lie #1:

I can't pray abandon because I fear that God will hurt me. Jesus prayed Take This Cup and Not My Will and God hurt *him*.

But because God hurt Jesus, he won't hurt us. Pastor Tim Keller fastens a hammock of hope over the canyon of abandon, writing, "Jesus got the scorpion and the snake so that we could have food at the Father's table. He received the sting and venom of death in our place. . . . We know that God will answer us when we call 'my God' because God did not answer Jesus when he made the same petition on the cross. For Jesus, the 'heavens were as brass'; he got the Great Silence so we could know that God hears and answers. We should ask God for things with boldness and specificity, with ardor, honesty, and diligence, yet with patient submission to God's will and wise love. All because of Jesus, and all in his name."[4]

The "hurt" we fear in abandon is a pain that God himself has carried. He carefully feeds it out so that we (and our world) might be better as we discover our need for him and crack open the windows and doors of our beings to allow him more entrance.

Maybe praying abandon will not cause God to "hurt" me, but rather will slice open my hurt places so that God can inhabit them with healing.

I take one baby step closer to the right side, to abandon.

Lie #2:

But what if God doesn't really love me? Not so much because he is not loving, but because I am not lovable? How can I dare to pray the abandon of Not My Will? What will happen to me when God is put in charge of the awfulness of me in my abandon?

I love the writing of Canadian farmer's wife, Ann Voskamp. (As she's become a friend over the years, I've come to love *her* as well!) One night, when her husband unexpectedly massaged her feet, she wondered, "Why is it so hard to receive? Why is it so hard to believe you are believed in? Why is it easier to pour out than to let yourself be loved? . . . Letting yourself receive love means trusting you will be loved in your vulnerable need; it means believing you are worthy of being loved. Why can that be so heartbreakingly hard?"[5]

I know why: because I know what's inside me. The pride. The selfishness. What I did yesterday. The things I thought—just an hour ago.

Stop it now. God *is* love. And our vulnerable God opens himself to cover my love-fears with himself. Love is not about my worthiness, my enoughness. It's about God's unendingness. And his desire to provide ongoing, everlasting connection with us. "For God so loved the world that he gave his one and only Son, that whoever believes in him shall not perish but have eternal life" (John 3:16).

I turn from fear. I open to love.
But then comes one more lie.

Lie #3:

What if God, really, is not good? Beyond our understanding. Beyond our comprehension? The abandon prayer of Not My Will would make suicidal sense in such a case.

Here, from this filthy pit of twisted thinking, is where Satan emerged in Eden to address Eve: "Did God really say, 'You must not eat from any tree in the garden?'" (Genesis 3:1) *Hiissssss! How can a good God not want you to eat of the delicious tree?* "You will not certainly die," the serpent said to the woman. "For God knows that when you eat from it your eyes will be opened, and you will be like God, knowing good and evil" (Genesis 3:4–5). *Hiissssss! God is not good—or he would want you to be like him.*

Gulp, gulp, gulp. We devour the lies, swallowing them down into our very beings where they merge and integrate, silently morphing into a new reality. One we cross-stitch and hang above our mental mantels.

Likely, it was this same untruth that tried to coil itself around Jesus during his garden prayer. *God will hurt you! God does not love you! God is not good! Take this cup!* But in Jesus' prayer coin, his honest Take This Cup answered the hiss with solid abandon: Not My Will. This was not an auto-abandon, where Jesus' divinity tipped the scales to surrender and the human part lost its grip.

No, Jesus' prayer comes in the midst of the same doubts we face, yet with a choice to yield to the love that conquers fear, never fails, and is always good. Jesus prayed a prayer of absolute abandon because he knew the Father loved him and he trusted and loved the Father back. I lift my pen again. I've been honest—oh, so honest. I know that God hears my honest requests and receives my honest expression of them. I yield to his goodness. I embrace his presence in my fears. I let him love me.

Not my will. I write it firmly and then set my pen aside for a moment, letting the moment sink in, waiting. *Maybe I want to love you through your family,* I sense God saying. *Maybe they need to love you in a way that you wouldn't allow without letting them come yet closer. Maybe there is something for each one of you in this unexpected unemployment. Something you could miss if you reject this season and what it might bring.*

I abandon.

Then back to the left I go! In seconds, more honest is pouring out. *But, Lord, you can still provide a job and this may never happen!*

And once again to the right. *Yes, of course,* he answers. *All things are possible with me. Are you willing to let me love your loved ones in whatever I provide? Are you willing to let me love you?*

The Gain of Abandon

Anne Lamott writes about the abandon prayer, "It begins with stopping in our tracks, or with our backs against the wall, or when we are going under the waves, or when we are just so sick and tired of being psychically sick and tired that we surrender, or at least we finally stop running away and at long last walk or lurch or crawl toward something."[6]

Abandon can be *hard*. In fact, real abandon is *usually* hard. Next to impossible. We drag our heels while being pulled in the opposite of our desired direction. We scrape our fingernails across the table as we're hulked by the waist out of our comfortable and familiar chair "We hold on so tightly to the good that we do know," Richard Foster writes, "that we cannot receive the greater good that we do not know."[7]

There are some stuck places where only the choice to abandon to apparent suffering can unstick us. Richard Rohr observes, "Suffering is the only thing strong enough to destabilize the imperial ego."[8]

Yet abandon brings its own rewards. Foster refers to abandon as relinquishment and relinquishment as the crucifixion, not the obliteration, of the will . . . and notes that crucifixion always has resurrection tied to it."[9] He goes on to say that "obedience has a way of strengthening rather than depleting our resources. If we obey in one small corner, we will have power to obey elsewhere. Obedience begets obedience."[10]

My friend and neighbor, Patricia Raybon, cracks her heart open in her book on prayer, *I Told the Mountain to Move*. In one story, she reveals her dismay when her raised-in-the-Christian-church daughter reveals she's become Muslim and is marrying a practicing Muslim. In a journey of prayer coin dimensions, Patricia shares how she felt challenged to pray, "Bless this or blow it up!" regarding the marriage.[11]

That's abandoned!

Abandoned to Abandon

I finished Facetiming again with Evan and collapsed in the apartment kitchen with a bolstering "cuppa," as Aussies call it. I sat marveling at how human we all are, whether in the States or Down Under.

In dinged a text from my Australian host, Terry, asking if we could meet for lunch. Having landed not quite twenty-four hours before, I'd researched return flights and settled on one that left in another twenty-four, just after the first conference. But I felt such turmoil about letting down the team that had brought me so far. Once home in Denver, would I be able to come back for the second conference? Should I?

Terry's eyes met mine across the cafe table as I picked at my salad and listed the elements of why I should stay—how I would be okay, how I was committed. Operating out of CEO Elisa mode, where I soldiered on to please others and meet their expectations, I continued my catalog of suggested sacrifices. Somewhere I slipped in a sentence that, of course, I realized that Evan might die. *What was I saying?* The words stung my heart. I hadn't really faced that before.

I noticed Terry wasn't eating. In fact, he wasn't talking. I was the only one doing that. He was waiting.

Oh, it struck me, *I'm doing the American Leader thing, the Soldier Elisa thing. I'm taking charge. Maybe I should be quiet a few minutes and allow Terry to . . . lead.*

Not my will.

I asked what he was thinking. Terry took a breath and very clearly told me that he and his entire team thought I should go home. On the very flight I'd selected. And not come back. They would video my talks and play them at the next venue the following weekend. They believed I needed to be with Evan.

In that moment, twenty-nine million pounds of anxiety lifted off my shoulders. Yes! I was going home! In less than forty-eight hours I would be back with Evan!

But new worries emerged. Take this cup! Would I make it home in time?

Not my will.

Oh, the manacles that chain us to our way! Fear of what God might allow, that he might hurt us. Concerns that he might not, after all, really love us. Hollow beliefs that he might not be good. We cling to our self-made safety, terrified to risk embracing the freedom he holds out for us.

God hurt Jesus so that he might not hurt us. God gave Jesus to demonstrate his love for us. God is good enough to love us as we are and yet not leave us this way.

Abandon is a journey of baby steps—away from the lies that shackle us in brokenness and toward the hope of healing. We learn from honest what it is we really want. We fall into the arms of abandon in order to receive it.

In utter reality, we beg, plead, and wail about what we want until we collapse in abandon to what God wants. To what he wants for us. Because somehow we've come to understand that what he wants is what, ultimately, we want as well.

• • •

"We all have a Gethsemane—that is a place and time in our lives when we face sorrow on the deepest level—a place of crisis, grief, anguish, excruciating pain, and loss. It's a time of separation, a tearing, or the ending of a relationship with someone or something that causes us to stop in our spiritual tracks and look more closely at who we are, our circumstances, and those around us. It brutally exposes what we honestly believe to be true in regard to God and his Word."
LESLIE MONTGOMERY[12]

• • •

"I am learning that there is a peace when I pray 'Not my will' with sincerity, but fear jumps in rather quickly. This is hard work!"
LYNETTE

CHAPTER 8

Jesus' Pivot—
The Space Between Honest and Abandon

> *". . . take this cup from me;*
> **yet** *not my will, but yours be done."*
> *Luke 22:42*

Take This Cup. Not My Will. Jesus prays *both* sides of the prayer coin. In a single sentence. He prays honest because he knows the Father loves him and will hear him. He prays abandon because he loves the Father and trusts his will. But how does Jesus switch from one to the other? On the heels of such an honest Take This Cup, how does he move to an abandoned Not My Will? From "what I want" to "what do *you* want, Father?" And how does he stay there, in abandon, all the way to the cross?

Notice the space between honest and abandon. Between Take This Cup and Not My Will. Just a smidge of a pause? Or is it more a chasm of hesitation? While Jesus' garden prayer tarried through the night, we aren't given the duration of the space in which he turned from the cry of honest to the surrender of abandon.

But there is a space.

Matthew, Mark, and Luke all report Jesus using a tiny word to hinge the two sides of his garden prayer—*yet*, sometimes translated "but" or "nevertheless." This conjunction connects two conflicting thoughts that are both valid. Take This Cup. Not My Will. Both true. Both necessary. Both mattering. *Yet*, this conjunction carves out a space where Jesus moves from the first thought to the second. And given the number of times he's reported to have repeated this prayer, perhaps even back and forth between them.

What happens in that space between honest and abandon? Is it similar to the psalmist's use of the Hebrew word *selah*, causing readers to stop and consider what was just said, as well as to anticipate what is to come? What stops Jesus and then starts him again? What occupies this turning point, this change of direction between the two sides of his prayer?

I picture a gymnast, tumbling across an inches-wide balance beam, leaping into the air and then landing again at the end of the sixteen-foot beam, her chalked feet searching out solid positioning. She locks her pose, back arched and arms stretched upward, like a swan drying her wings. Then, decisively, she spins around, suddenly facing the opposite direction. Pivoting.

Or maybe a basketball player, precisely catching a pass and then quickly pivoting to aim and shoot—*swish!*

A pivot. A rotation. A turn. A spin in a different direction. A flip of the prayer coin.

Take This Cup—*yet*—Not My Will.

I suppose the space might not be quite so quickly bridged. For Jesus, it could have been more of a process. Perhaps he pivoted, did an about-face, and then repeated pivots until his whole being was headed in a new direction.

However it happened for Jesus, something occurred in that space between honest and abandon—something that moved him from Take This Cup to Not My Will.

In the Pivot of Prayer: Answers

Could it be that God answered his Take This Cup prayer? Is that why Jesus could seemingly and seamlessly pivot from honest to abandon?

Some say no, suggesting this garden prayer is the only one the Father did not answer in Jesus' earthly life. In his book *Prayer: Does It Make Any Difference?* Philip Yancey concludes, "Not even Jesus was exempt from unanswered prayer."[1] Pastor and author Tim Keller, meanwhile, believes that "Jesus' prayers were given the rejection that we sinners merit so that our prayers could have the reception that he merits."[2] Oh, so true. Still others suggest that Jesus actually withdrew his prayer in relinquishment to abandon as he so delighted in doing the will of the Father.[3]

While the Father did not ultimately remove the cup from the lips of his Son, Hebrews 5:7 underlines that Jesus' prayer was certainly heard: "During the days of Jesus' life on earth, he offered up prayers and petitions with fervent cries and tears to the one who could save him from death, and he was heard because of his reverent submission."

Okay . . . Jesus' prayer was heard. But was it "answered"?

Think about what Jesus had requested: Take this cup. As we've considered, he likely was requesting a total removal of the torture, humiliation, pain, and separation from the Father that the cross (and the events leading up to it) would bring. Completely human, Jesus leaned honest.

Perhaps the Father heard his Son's prayer and answered in part. Luke tells us that God sent an angel to attend to Jesus, strengthening him in a moment where he had no remaining human strength (Luke 22:43). Some early commentators suggested that God saved Jesus from immediate death in the garden before his eventual death on the cross and the completion of his destiny.[4] In addition, three days after Jesus died on the cross, the Father raised him back to life, saving him from eternal death and everlasting separation from the Father.[5] As Hebrews 5:7 says, "Jesus prayed to the one who could save him from death," and the Father answered him. He "took the cup" of eternal death from his beloved Son.

Indeed, answered prayer played a role in the pivot of Jesus' garden prayer. Perhaps Jesus flipped the prayer coin from Take This Cup to Not My Will because God partially answered his plea, strengthening him to move from honest to the other side of the prayer coin—abandon.

In the Pivot of Prayer: Intimacy

Was there more at work in that space between honest and abandon that motivated Jesus' pivot? A more layered element of relationship? I rehearse again my discovery that prayer creates honesty which develops trust and results in surrender. A risk resulting in a surprising peace that invites further yielding.

Turning to the last gospel in my Bible, I'm struck by John's toe touch on Jesus' garden prayer. "Shall I not drink the cup the Father has given me?" (John 18:11).

As is his custom, John tends to include elements of testimony about Jesus that the three synoptic writers exclude. John's summary of Jesus' final night on earth includes five chapters (13–17) of the discourse in which Jesus prays to be glorified, prays for his disciples, and prays for future believers—which includes you and me. John 18:1 tells us that when Jesus had finished praying, most likely the long prayer we see in the preceding chapter, he "left with his disciples and crossed the Kidron Valley. On the other side there was a garden, and he and his disciples went into it." Though John doesn't say it here, this would seem to be the spot where Jesus prayed his prayer coin of Take This Cup and Not My Will.

John doesn't even mention a struggle. No hint whatsoever of any turmoil in the heart of the Savior. Zero. Theologian D. A. Carson believes John is emphasizing the *outcome* of Jesus' garden prayer in Jesus' "firm resolution to accept what the Father gives him . . . (rather) than the agonizing supplication that secured it."[6]

In John's one-sentence summary, Jesus seems so settled. In fact, in the last sentence of each of the gospel writers' telling, Jesus appears reconciled, almost peacefully so, to the will of the Father. So how did Jesus arrive at this outcome? Yes, it appears the Father at least partially answered Jesus' prayer. But did something else happen in the space between honest and abandon?

I read and reread John's chapters looking for clues, struck by how very *connected* the Son is with the Father:

- "Jesus knew that the hour had come for him to leave this world *and go to the Father*" (John 13:1).

- "Jesus knew that the Father had put all things under his power, and that he *had come from God and was returning to God*" (John 13:3).

- "Jesus said, '*Now the Son of Man is glorified and God is glorified in him*. If God is glorified in him, God will glorify the Son in himself, and will glorify him at once" (John 13:31).

- "Jesus answered, 'I am the way and the truth and the life. No one comes to the Father except through me. *If you really know me, you will know my Father as well. From now on, you do know him and have seen him*'" (John 14:6–7).

- "*Anyone who has seen me has seen the Father*. How can you say, 'Show us the Father'? *Don't you believe that I am in the Father, and that the Father is in me?* The words I say to you I do not speak on my own authority. *Rather, it is the Father, living in me, who is doing his work. Believe me when I say that I am in the Father and the Father is in me*; or at least believe on the evidence of the works themselves" (John 14:9–11).

- "*These words you hear are not my own; they belong to the Father who sent me*" (John 14:24).

- "As the Father has loved me, so have I loved you. Now remain in my love. If you keep my commands, you will remain in my love, just as *I have kept my Father's commands and remain in his love*" (John 15:9–10).

- "*All that belongs to the Father is mine*" (John 16:15).

- "*I came from the Father and entered the world; now I am leaving the world and going back to the Father*" (John 16:28).

- "I have brought you glory on earth by finishing the work you gave me to do. *And now, Father, glorify me in your presence with the glory I had with you before the world began*" (John 17:4–5).

- "I pray for them. I am not praying for the world, but for those you have given me, for they are yours. *All I have is yours, and all you have is mine*" (John 17:9–10).

I keep reading and realize that Jesus is praying, layer after layer, that his disciples—both then and now and through all time to come—would be connected to each other and to him in the way he is connected to the Father.

- "Holy Father, protect them by the power of your name, the name you gave me, *so that they may be one as we are one*" (John 17:11).

- "*My prayer is not for them* [the original Eleven] *alone. I pray also for those who will believe in me through their message, that all of them may be one, Father, just as you are in me and I am in you.* May they also be in us so that the world may believe that you have sent me. I have given them the glory that you gave me, *that they may be one as we are one—I in them and you in me—so that they may be brought to complete unity. Then the world will know that you sent me and have loved them even as you have loved me*" (John 17:20–23).

Connected in relationship. Intimately so. One with the Father. The unity Jesus desires for his disciples mirrors the unity he possesses with the Father. It's a relationship that includes the accomplishment of mission from the motivation of love, the wealth of love that ties him and the Father together. It's a relationship that Jesus enjoyed in that moment and enjoys today. It's a relationship that he died to make possible for us to enter as well.

And I sense the true source of Jesus' pivot. The space between honest and abandon, between Take This Cup and Not My Will, and between "what I want" and "what God wants" is filled to full with the purest love that comes from unity. Jesus is one with the Father, intimately so. His ultimate goal is that we—you and I—would be one with the Father just as he is. And he wants us to invite others into this relationship of unity as well.

In the Pivot of Prayer: Alignment

Jesus pivots as his prayer is partly answered and he is strengthened. Jesus pivots because he is united in love with the Father. And also . . . I begin to see that this two-sided expression works in Jesus to *align* him to God's will. It is more than simply submitting.

Be clear, it's not that Jesus suddenly whipped his will into easy submission. Matthew, Mark and Luke all mention Jesus "crying out" on the cross (Matthew 27:50; Mark 15:37; Luke 23:46). The words used actually mean he screamed.[7] Ann Voskamp pens, "Jesus died crying,"[8] Jesus' pain continues. But this two-sided coin of prayer is a loving tool of the Father's work in the life of the Son.

Richard Rohr writes, "Prayer must lead us beyond mind, words, and ideas to a more spacious place where God has a chance to get in."[9]

Yes.

The space between honest and abandon is the space where "God has a chance to get in." To align the heart of the Son with the will of the Father. Even though Son and Father are already connected. Even though they are already one. When the completely human Son struggles with a will somehow divergent from the one he divinely shares with the Father, the intimacy of their relationship allows Jesus to pivot from honest to abandon. Through this process, Jesus eventually arrives in a place where the oneness he actually possesses with the Father is the oneness he feels.

Until the intimacy of his prayer coin can carry him up to, through, and beyond the cross. *Take this cup, yet not my will.*

Regarding coins, there is actually a third "side": the edge. The edges of some world coins carry designs like vines; in the United States, dimes and quarters feature reeds (parallel ridges) and some dollar coins even carry the phrase E Pluribus Unum on their edge.

How is the third side of a coin formed? By a third die, called the "collar," which holds the blank in place during the minting. The pressure of the striking on the obverse and reverse imprints the edge of the coin with the design from the collar.[10]

If we see Jesus' prayer as a two-sided coin of honest and abandon, we might also notice a message of ongoing intimacy imprinted around the edge.

The prayer coin is all about intimacy. Every bit of it. The honest and the abandon. The struggling against and the settling in. God isn't the road. He's not the cosmic Santa. The place of pivot between honest and abandon is the place we discover all that we have most sought and desired and *yearned for* our whole lives.

• • •

*"The whole reason why we pray is
to be united into the vision and
contemplation of him to whom we pray."*
JULIAN OF NORWICH[11]

• • •

*"For me, it's all about trust and taking it
to the next level with God. I know that I can
trust him, yet I'm afraid of the pain that
inevitably accompanies any type of growth."*
KRISTINE

CHAPTER 9

Our Pivot—
The Space Between Honest
and Abandon

". . . take this cup from me;
yet *not my will, but yours be done."*
Luke 22:42

Over the past months of writing this manuscript, the pages of my prayer journal have filled to full. I open back to those days when I first began and then decided to extend my exploration. In hindsight, I can see so very much discovery.

My first prayer coin attempts included this entry from February 3:

Take This Cup

- *I'm burdened. Evan's meetings in Australia and the opportunity to accompany him played a large role in my accepting this faraway and time-consuming speaking engagement. Now he can't go, and I'm headed out on my own. Really? Take this cup!*

- *Will I connect with Evan's team and with the women I'll be speaking to?*
- *Will the kids or Evan need me when I'm so far away?*

Not My Will

- *Australia is your deal, God, in your timing. You knew this would happen—that Evan would not be able to go after we made plans for me to accept the engagement. Not my will.*
- *Help me trust you with how my messages will fit this audience. They are your women.*
- *Help me trust you with Evan and the kids.*
- *Help me to see you provide for me on the journey.*
- *Help me watch for you in the in-between week at the beach, to meet and restore me.*
- *Help me to let you use me.*

Then, after returning to the States and Evan, I reviewed the twirling prayer coin days of Take This Cup and Not My Will during the crisis of Australia, chronicling my cumulative honest and abandon reflections.

Take This Cup

- *At first, I didn't want to go to Australia alone. I didn't want the "waste" of a week between the conferences. I didn't want to leave Evan recovering from surgery alone.*
- *Then, when the crisis hit, I didn't want to be so*

far away. I didn't want Evan to be so sick. I didn't want to disappoint women who had planned to attend a conference with me there in person and would find out I wasn't. At the same time, I didn't want to go back to Denver and then have to return to Australia just a few days later.

Not My Will

- *Going to Australia alone set up an opportunity for you, Lord, to work in ways I couldn't have imagined otherwise:*
  - *We had to ask the kids to step up. How dear they were! Their offers and gestures bubbled up from the well of their own love languages. Ethan wanted to take Evan homemade food. Eva wanted to bring a cozy blanket because his teeth chattered. Evan received each sincere offering with a grateful heart.*
  - *We were all forced to take one more step to face our mortality.*
  - *While I doubt that Evan was "helped" by being alone, if he had to be, at least he was in ICU, where he received round-the-clock care, rather than in a normal hospital room.*

- *I didn't have to return to Australia, Lord. You met the needs of the women at the second conference through the prerecorded videos. I was able to Skype in at the beginning of their gathering and you gave me the message to give them. While I couldn't be there in person, you were there in Person.*

After several more days, Evan was released to continue intravenous antibiotics at home. Eventually the infection was resolved, and Evan's leg healed. He walks normally today. He has no disability. I don't "take care of him." And while this health ordeal was one of the greatest challenges we've yet seen, the real takeaway has been the lesson of the prayer coin. Learning to pray with honest abandon. Both.

It's a lot to consider praying Take This Cup *and* Not My Will. We tend to slip into one side or the other.

Take this cup. Take this cup. Take this cup. In honest blurts, we hurl our emotions and needs and wants at God and get up and go. But when we pray only "take this cup," do we ever really join God and what he wants to do in our days?

Or, we pray "not my will." Not my will. Not my will. Not my will. We submit our desires to God's, barely even acknowledging that we *have* desires. Robotically, we obey and "praise Jesus" after every sentence, swallowing some notion that, somehow, our unplugged hearts please him because we're "doing the right thing."

We tend to pray, "Take this cup *or* not my will."

But what about, "Take this cup *yet* not my will"? Might that be a tool of the Father's work in the lives of his sons and daughters? Just as Jesus saw his Take This Cup prayer answered, at least in part, might we be strengthened in the same way? Just as Jesus, out of love for and trust in his Father, pivoted between the two sides of the coin, might we? And just as the Father aligned the will of Jesus to his own through the prayer coin, might he align ours?

Our Pivot Discoveries

What might we discover about Jesus, about ourselves, and about God if we pendulum-swung our personal prayers right between Take This Cup and Not My Will? What if we teeter-tottered our utterances between vulnerable, raw honesty and yielded, surrendered abandon while our *relationship* with God grew clearer, more and more *real*?

I'm learning that this prayer coin—praying with honest *yet* abandon—offers tangible help for our problems with prayer.

Think about it. Praying honest before God—about what we want and don't want—gives us strength to abandon to what God wants. Telling him what we *really* want helps us to admit that to ourselves. When we do, we're able to see that in many ways what we want is less than, not as good as, what he wants. So can we abandon our wants for God's.

My daughter has been challenged in the world of childbirth. Many pregnancies with only one boy to show for it. A marvelous boy, I'll give you. But just one. I remember well the morning she called to share that she and her husband had decided to try for another baby. Again.

My heart seized up and I choked out my concerns. She'd already endured so much! Miscarriage. A silent delivery at just twenty-two weeks. "Why do you want to go through this?" I blurted. *Take this cup!*

She responded, "Mom, if you're not going to be supportive, I won't be able to share this with you, however it turns out."

I reflected on my marvelous grand "one," now my adored play-and-soul mate. I did not want to miss *anything* in a future grand.

So I pivoted. *Not my will.*

The process began, the monthly charting and calculating and doctoring and checking. Month after month ticked past. Easter rolled around, the very holiday when, several decades prior, Evan and I had been informed that we would become parents of our daughter through adoption. Now, decades later, I prayed yet again for my daughter to become pregnant. My Take This Cup of not wanting her to risk a difficult pregnancy had pivoted to Not My Will, and had in turn become a Take This Cup of asking God to remove infertility. I spurted out a prayer: *I'm pretty sure that she's not going to fall in love with you through more suffering, God. I'm pretty sure she needs to see your goodness and love. Give her a baby . . . please?*

As the holiday ebbed and the sun rose on a new week, my daughter returned to the doctor to discover she was, indeed, pregnant. Today we tumble through life with two grandboys—more than a decade apart in age, but brothers nonetheless. I look back at my daughter's desire and at my Take This Cup/Not My Will struggle with it.

I see both sides of the prayer coin at work and the pivot that tipped me from one to the other.

Philip Yancey confesses our struggle: "I need the corrective vision of prayer because all day long I will lose sight of God's perspective. . . . Prayer, and only prayer, restores my vision to one that more resembles God's."[1]

The prayer coin works for every important issue of life.

Take This Cup: Please keep my teenage children safe. Protect them from poor choices.

Yet . . . (we pivot)

Not My Will: Help me to trust that even if they make poor choices, you can use those choices to help them see their need for you.

Take This Cup: I'm embarrassed by my children's choices, Lord. Oh, take this cup of my being evaluated by their actions!

Yet . . . (we pivot)

Not My Will: Their choices don't define my value. Help me understand that you don't judge or evaluate me by my children's choices. You evaluate me by how I love you, and how I express my love for you in responding to my children's choices.

Take This Cup: Give me a spouse.

Yet . . . (we pivot)

Not My Will: Help me to see that *you* are my spouse. May I learn to let you love me. May I learn to love you more.

Take This Cup: But I'm so lonely! I long for a soul
 mate with "skin on." Take this loneliness.
Yet . . . (we pivot)
Not My Will: When I feel lonely, help me to invite
 you into the loneliness, to be with me even here.

Take This Cup: I want that job.
Yet . . . (we pivot)
Not My Will: Help me to trust you to provide for my
 needs. Help me be open to the job you have for
 me—to shape me and use me in the lives of others.

Take This Cup: I don't really want to work—I want
 you to just take care of me.
Yet . . . (we pivot)
Not My Will: Help me understand that you shape
 and grow me through work—and you have called
 me to shape others for you in the workplace.

Day after day. Issue building on issue. Struggle layered on struggle. Back and forth between honest Take This Cup and Not My Will abandon. I grow more honest before God and therefore more abandoned to his will because I'm more honest. Then the more we abandon to God, the freer—safer—we are to be honest with God. The more honest we are about what we don't want, the freer we become to abandon what we want for what he wants. When we choose what God wants, we are able to see—more honestly—more of what we want. Things we don't know we want until we decide we really want what he wants, whatever that might be.

Oneness increases.

Abiding with God

This oneness, this intimacy that God craves and we were created for, can be expressed by the concept of *abiding*. Before Jesus prayed for both his first-century and future-century disciples—that they would all be one as he and the Father are one (John 17:21)—he invited all to abide in him (John 15). The verb, translated in the New International Version as "remain," holds the concept of being united with, one with, and joined together, and to remain in place or stay.

Before praying the prayer coin, before praying in the upper room, Jesus taught his disciples the concept of oneness that comes through remaining in relationship with him and the Father.

> "Remain in me, as I also remain in you. No branch can bear fruit by itself; it must remain in the vine. Neither can you bear fruit unless you remain in me.
>
> "I am the vine; you are the branches. If you remain in me and I in you, you will bear much fruit; apart from me you can do nothing. If you do not remain in me, you are like a branch that is thrown away and withers; such branches are picked up, thrown into the fire and burned. If you remain in me and my words remain in you, ask whatever you wish, and it will be done for you. This is to my Father's glory, that you bear much fruit, showing yourselves to be my disciples.
>
> "As the Father has loved me, so have I loved you. Now remain in my love" (John 15:4–9).

God the Father used the pivot of Jesus' prayer coin to woo him toward the cross. And the Father makes the pivot a loving tool in the lives of his children, aligning us to his desires rather than demanding obedience. Abiding, or remaining in relationship, is our response to God's shaping of our desires and wills to match his own. Ultimately, God wants us to want what he wants because he wants us to want *him*.

Oneness with God

Jesus prayed both sides of the prayer coin, pivoting between honest and abandon, because he possessed oneness with the Father. Jesus prayed that we would be one, as he and his Father are one (John 17:21). One with God and eventually one with each other. But note here—oneness with God is what creates oneness with each other.

Did you get that? *Oneness with God is what creates oneness with each other.*

It seems to me that intimacy is the key here. Popular author Beth Moore writes, "Prayer keeps us in constant communion with God, which is the goal of our entire believing lives . . . the ultimate goal God has for us is not power but personal intimacy with Him."[2] Being one with God is what allows us to pivot between the two sides of the prayer coin.

This space between honest and abandon, this pivoting, becomes God's tool to develop his longed-for intimacy. Which becomes our longed-for intimacy as well.

Pivoting happens because of intimacy and intimacy continues because of pivoting.

We want what we want. Okay, make that we want what we *think* we want. But when we honestly confess what we want to God, we become able to see what he wants. And when we see what he wants, we can change what we want.

Sometimes the space between honest and abandon is actually larger than either one, carving out a new place to be in tension and yet one with God. This "middle voice,"[3] as Eugene Peterson calls it, becomes the space of true transformation. Richard Foster picks up this theme in his book, *Prayer: Finding the Heart's True Home* and explains, "In grammar the active voice is when we take action, and the passive voice is when we receive the action of another, but in the middle voice, we both act and are acted upon. We participate in the formation of the action and reap the benefits of it."[4] In this pivot, God works on our hearts to pry them away from our understanding and mold them toward his.

This middle space where we let God work is sacred. And like abandon, pivoting is hard work. We teeter between wanting what *we* want and wanting what *God* wants. Like Jesus, we gather up our split beings and knit ourselves back into one seamless offering.

Intimacy with God

At this stage in our lives, Evan and I are somewhat surprised that our family consists of the two of us and two giant dogs. Darla is a purebred Rottweiler we inherited at age three from our son. Now nearly eleven years old, she is diabetic and blind and needs careful supervision. We rescued Wilson, a Rottie wannabe, when he was about the same age as young Darla. Both of these big babies, as our dogsitter refers to them, are dear to us—and a lot of dog to manage. When we leave our house for any long period, we put them in the "tile room," a basement area that is pretty much indestructible. It's better for us and it's better for them, if you know what I mean.

One afternoon I pottied the dogs, put them in the tile room, and headed out to run some errands. But, just seconds down the street, I realized I'd left my cell phone and turned around. When I entered the house from the garage, retracing my steps to find my phone, I paused, trying to identify an unexpected noise. An eerie croon. Coming from the basement. Not a bark, not a whine. A howl? I opened the basement door and stood at the top of the stairs listening. Yes . . . it was definitely howling.

What on earth? I'd *just* left them minutes before! What was wrong?

I hurried down the stairs and then caught myself at the bottom. Watching the dogs through the glass of the tile room door, I took in the sight of my two big babies. At a hundred pounds apiece, they sat erect with their necks extended, noses pointed to the ceiling, howling.

Aaarrrrruuuuuueooohhhhh! Eeeeooooowwwwhhhh! Yeeeeeooooooowwwwww!

One would breathe in and the other would sing out, taking turns in their canine chorus.

I laughed. (Who wouldn't?) They were so forlorn. So miserable. So lonesome and yearning. It was heartbreaking—and also funny. Silly puppies!

"Guys!" I opened the door and their howling ceased as they turned surprised faces toward me, blind Darla looking just off-target as always. "You're okay. I'm right here. I'll be back. Don't freak out."

They obediently circled their beds, settling in to wait for my return as I headed back up the stairs to resume my errands. Driving down the street, I couldn't help but wonder if they always howled when I left. Bless their hearts! My insides tugged a bit at the thought.

In that moment, I sensed God near. *Elisa*, he seemed to say, *that's how I feel when you leave me.*

I gasped. I mean really, I had no idea! That intense? Surely not pathetically forlorn like my dogs, but an undeniable yearning. For me. Just as God searched for Adam in Eden, calling out to him, "Where are you?" (Genesis 3:9)

The howling echoed, this time with a divine intonation. *Aaarrrruuuuuueoooohhhh! Eeeeooooowwwhhh! Yeeeeeooooooowwwwww!* God feels that way when I leave him?

Words from Richard Foster move me:

The heart of God is an open wound of love. He aches over our distance and preoccupation. He mourns that we do not draw near to him. He grieves that we have forgotten him. He weeps over our obsession with muchness and manyness. He longs for our presence.

And he is inviting you—and me—to come home, to come home to where we belong, to come home to that for which we were created.[5]

Later, that night, I pulled open my journal—not the prayer coin journal but the regular one where I write down quotes and such—and read, "God . . . rushes to us at the first hint of our openness. He is the hound of heaven baying relentlessly upon our track."[6]

They haunt me, those howls. God wants me to be with him that much? Why? Surely not because he's dependent on me or because he's bored, as my dogs might be. No, his desire for me is intentional. He *is* love and he made me to be loved. By him. Because he knows what he made me for. And he's bent on seeing me be that person.

In his classic work, *Our Prayer*, Louis Evely suggests, "Prayer is offering ourselves to God so that he may have a chance of doing in us what he is always wanting to do, but is prevented from doing by our going away before he has a chance to begin."[7]

Here, in the pivot between honest and abandon, God has a chance to work on us the way he's always wanted to. A chance to teach us. A chance to reveal himself to us. A chance to love us the way he's always wanted to. A chance to speak against the lies that hiss through our thinking, to replace them with the truth about his being. A chance to draw us into the intimacy he created us to experience—an intimacy that cannot be discovered any other way, and once discovered, cannot be denied.

Yes, God wants to be with me—to love me—that

much. He is that honestly abandoned in my direction. And now comes the follow up question: will I be the same way with him? Will I let him love me? Will you?

• • •

Just as the gymnast and the basketball player learned their pivot through practice, we develop a prayer muscle memory through the process of pivoting over and over. As my friend J'Anne observes, "We are born in our beings to not be able to hold paradox. Jesus demonstrates that we can learn to. We can fully have this, and pivot, and fully have that."

Honest—pivot—abandon—pivot—honest—pivot— abandon. All yielding an intimacy that fuels further honest—pivot—abandon—pivot—honest—pivot— abandon . . . and more intimacy.

The prayer coin.

• • •

"But if God is so good as you represent Him, and if He knows all that we need, and better far than we do ourselves, why should it be necessary to ask Him for anything? I answer, What if He knows Prayer to be the thing we need first and most? What if the main object in God's idea of prayer be the supplying of our great, our endless need—the need of Himself? Hunger may drive the runaway child home, and he may or may not be fed at once, but he needs his mother more than his dinner. Communion with God is the one

_need of the soul beyond all other need: prayer
is the beginning of that communion, and some
need is the motive of that prayer. So begins a
communion, a talking with God, a coming-to-
one with Him, which is the sole end of prayer."_
GEORGE MACDONALD[8]

• • •

_"The two-sided prayer stirs up courage to
boldly return to the throne of grace with a bigger,
bolder request. Didn't see that coming!"_
PAT

CHAPTER 10

How to Pray
the Prayer Coin

". . . take this cup from me;
yet not my will, but yours be done."
Luke 22:42

That first day in Australia, shortly after I rose from my fetaled honesty on the floor of my bedroom in my home-away-from-home, I Facetimed yet again with Evan. Oh, I'd washed my face and gathered my being a bit so that Evan wouldn't be overly worried about his suddenly fragile wife. I knew I needed to pay attention to the medical details he would be sharing.

I shut the door of the bedroom for both quiet and privacy, and situated myself on the floor. In that moment, waiting for the connection, I took in my surroundings—a double bed and, above its headboard, a photograph of five stones positioned in a horizontal row. Was it aboriginal in origin? Something seemed familiar about it, but I couldn't place what.

My tablet beeped. When Evan's face came on the

screen, I joyed from within. Technology can be such a wonderful thing.

I listened as he explained the plan to flush specific intravenous antibiotics through his body to address the infection, which was indeed the dreaded necrotizing fasciitis. He just kind of slipped that piece of information into the same sentence with the treatment plan. I made Evan pause to let me absorb the idea. He went on to say that, during one of his therapies, his original ankle wound had been inadvertently opened—ever so slightly—but enough to allow the evil to enter.

We prayed together, agreed to talk again in another hour, and disconnected. My gaze returned to the photograph above the bed and I realized what was familiar about it. That morning I'd read in Luke 4 about Jesus' temptation in the wilderness. Something in Satan's cocky, mocking dare to the forty-day-fasting Jesus, "Tell this stone to become bread," echoed through me (Luke 4:3).

I shifted and considered the shepherd boy David palming the five smooth stone weapons he'd selected for his battle with Goliath. He would only need one rock to slay the beast. Yet God seemed to have provided backups.

I scanned the five stones in the photo, mentally assigning the first one on the left to Evan's IV. *May it work to kill the infection in his body! Just one stone! Take this cup! Yet . . . not my will, God. You know how many stones, and which ones, might be needed to heal Evan.*

As the days progressed, I spoke at the first conference, flew back home to nurse Evan, and finally Skyped with the second Australian venue. I thought of my two-sided prayer, and of God's provision of those stones. I had even emailed the metaphor to praying friends who joined me in asking God to use just one stone.

And God did. He used the one stone and my husband was healed.

Did my pivot between honest and abandon occur because of answered prayer? Or was my prayer answered because of the intimacy with my Father I was experiencing? Or was the whole honest and abandon ordeal purposed to align me (and Evan) to God's best desires—that we live in unity with him and with each other?

As I've shared, there were many, many steps of both honest and abandon in our Australian ordeal. This stone moment was just one more "take this cup, yet not my will" prayer. I'd already been pivoting between the two sides of the prayer coin in the everyday of my February. Then I'd prayed with an upped ante for the hours and days endured in crisis.

Principles of the Prayer Coin Practice

From that February prayer coin adventure and on up to today, Evan and I have learned much about the practice of this prayer. The prayer coin practice is just that: a practice. It's something we do over and over—and it's something that, as we practice, we get better at.

Shortly after I began this manuscript, I saw a good friend with whom I consult about ministry efforts and, especially, writing. Steve and I first met during my days as CEO of MOPS International, which he served as a consultant. A friendship formed, which soon included our spouses too. Since Steve lives way out west, we make it a habit to connect whenever he's in Colorado working with other companies.

One Monday afternoon we planned to meet at my favorite Mexican place. In preparation for our conversation, I'd sent him the first two chapters of this book, which he had promised to read on the plane. Of course they were in a very early stage, but the core concept was there. I was already dipping into the salsa when he slid into the booth, across the table from me.

Steve's face lit up with excitement. "I like this!" he announced. "The prayer coin—wow!" And in we dove, rehearsing the Synoptic Gospel tellings and John's follow-up and then teasing apart *honest* and *abandon* (was that the right word for the Not My Will side?) An hour or so later, we parted ways, with Steve heading off to the east coast for more meetings and me to Grand Rapids for *Discover the Word* radio work.

A few days later, early in the morning, an email arrived from Steve:

I cannot capture in words what happened last night (well, actually this morning), but let me give you the gist of it. . . .

Yesterday was an exhausting day of work. I went to bed at 9 p.m. (6 p.m. body time, as I was traveling out of my normal time zone). I awoke at 2 a.m. I tried to go back to sleep but couldn't. And then I prayed.

Yours is a dangerous prayer. For almost three hours I went back and forth between honest and abandon.

Intimacy is indeed the hook, the center. But so too is awe.

I now understand why Jesus stopped praying at one point and went to the disciples. This isn't a prayer where you go from honest to abandon and that's it. The abandon leads you back to the honest and back and forth as you get deeper into that intimacy.

At one point I got the connection that honest could be the modifier for abandon. I think of the phrase "wanton abandon," which I associate in the positive sense with being so in love, so enraptured, that you give yourself completely to the other. I think this gets at the intimacy of the piece.

I was praying that this close connection I was feeling with God would last, because such moments only linger for a second or two. And in the midst of that I had this sense of God essentially saying, "You can't handle more yet. You need to work your way up to this." Not in a legalistic way, but just a caring comment that I haven't literally spent that much time with God for a while . . . and that this kind of prayer requires practice.

Steve was one of the first who tried out the prayer coin concept in this depth. As I write this book, I'm working very hard to listen to the learnings of my husband, my church, and my praying friends like Steve to learn more about this practice. To be honest, I haven't *ever* prayed for three hours! When I first read Steve's comments, I felt intimidated, as you might be feeling right now. Hang in there. We all learn in our own ways and at our own pace.

As I've practiced the prayer coin, and as I've connected with the others who've taken the prayer dare to practice it, certain principles are beginning to stand out:

The prayer coin often begins as a crisis prayer.

The initial felt need of this prayer is urgent, a tug-of-war between what you and I want and what God wants. Just as Jesus crumpled at the crossroads between the garden and the cross, we topple in our moments of suffering: A cancer diagnosis. Death. Bankruptcy. Divorce. A child's belligerent turning away from health and home. Disaster. "Take this cup, yet not my will" offers the honest expression of our suffering while abandoning ourselves to the only One who truly loves enough to provide what is ultimately best for us.

A prayer coin novice wrote me:

> *I'm finding that I want what I want so much! It's all I can utter! I beg and plead and pound the door before God. Take this cup! And then I want what God wants so much! I yield and slip down to receive. For my son. For my daughter. For my spouse. For my world.*

The prayer coin is also an everyday prayer.

By practicing this prayer daily, our spiritual muscles strengthen, equipping us to embrace the intimacy God designed us to enjoy. Take this cup. Honestly, this is what I want, God. Yet . . . not my will.

What do you want? In your marriage? In your lack of marriage? With your children? With your childlessness?

In your work? In your lack of work? The daily turning of the prayer coin from honest to abandon becomes a rhythmic relationship, one in which we are utterly convinced that we are never alone and always loved.

A friend's comment reinforced this idea:

At first it seemed like honest and abandon were best used for the big issues. But increasingly I've found in them a natural transition into my daily prayers. I'm mindful of the need for both honest and abandon, but the transition between them seems less dramatic—and the cadence or rhythm becomes more routine without it diminishing the power of the duality of this prayer.

And from another:

There's a point where you reach abandon and you need to let it go. Other times, I feel I'm like James 1—you know, "the waves on the sea." I do need to return to Not My Will when I start holding onto my desires again, even after I've surrendered them. But for many issues, those are good and done. All this to say the obvious: this isn't intended to be the only way you pray.

The prayer coin is a cumulative prayer.

The two-sided prayer coin builds on itself. Honest leads to abandon. Abandon leads back to more honest. More honest flips into more abandon. And so it goes, side to side, pivoting in an intimacy that becomes more unified so that eventually all that can be seen is the spinning coin of an unbroken relationship.

In came another email from a friend trying out the prayer coin practice:

I've been separating the two sides, as if they're individual prayers. First the honest, then the abandon. But the more I practice this prayer, those two are melding. Hard to explain this, but I'm finding that honest is more than asking for what I want—it's wrestling with the question, "Am I totally honest with myself about what I want?" Part of "Thy will be done" is almost a plea to make my own request more refined, since I may not even know my own heart.

In his book *Knowing the Face of God*, Tim Stafford writes, "We do not pray to tell God what he does not know, nor to remind him of things he has forgotten. He already cares for the things we pray about. . . . He has simply been waiting for us to care about them with him."[1]

Praying the prayer coin aligns us with God so that we are so integrated, so in congruence with his Being, so intimately connected that we want nothing other than what he wants. This is not a static state that we "reach" and then live from in fullness, but rather an ongoing discovery of both honest and abandon.

The prayer coin is both personal and communal.

The "Our Father" of the Lord's Prayer reminds us that God is surely our own, individual Abba. But as a body of believers, God is also our communal Father. We can pray "take this cup, yet not my will" as a group and discover the mystery of unity with God and also each other.

But one of my early readers points out that the "community" can be a very small (and important) one:

> It struck me that "*our Father*" wasn't just about "*our*" in the collective sense, how he's God and Father of every believer. Instead, I realized that it can also be read that "*our*" means Jesus and me. *Jesus is inviting me to pray in exactly the way he prayed.*

The prayer coin is a prayer of trust.

It's an all-out honest request and expression of what we want, coupled with an all-out abandon to what God wants. One friend's discovery mirrored many of the "but, but, but's" I'd thrown at God in my own prayer coin journal:

> *It's ultimately a journey from fear to trust, and not an easy journey. Normally, what I desire from prayer is peace or joy. But this morning, I found myself simply hungering for or lingering in or just wanting God's goodness. Part of that trust comes out of the recognition of that goodness.*
>
> *What God seemed to be saying to me this morning was pure and clear, and a little surprising. I prayed my "take this cup" and back came God's response in a simple question. "Do you trust me?"*

Our prayer life—and, ultimately, our entire relationship with God—comes down to trust. And we trust him because of his power and goodness, which we've seen in history and our own lives. As my friend Debbie says,

> *Many of us don't live on the resurrection side of this prayer but stay in the tug-of-war of the garden. Jesus moved on. Sometimes I sense God nudging me to get out of the garden. To recognize the short-term challenges but keep my focus on the long-term reality.*

And still another friend comments,

> *I feel like I only have so many issues that fit within the framework of honest and abandon at times and that by bringing these repeatedly to God is a bit like lifting up the plant from the soil to check and see how the roots are doing, instead of just trusting that indeed, it's growing.*

In the end, the prayer coin is a prayer of learning to trust God with the everyday and crisis matters of our everyday and crisis moments.

The prayer coin is a discipline.

My sweet friend Cindy responded with an insight I hadn't yet discovered:

> *I sense a huge movement in our Christian world of doing the left side of the page (Take This Cup) but not the right side (Not My Will). Our current trend is toward being all about love without any focus on sacrifice. We're still called to be obedient even when it doesn't necessarily feel loving. Obedience is love.*

The prayer coin practice teaches us the spiritual discipline of obedience, which grows us up. And one more thing: you can't do it fast. Practicing the prayer coin usually takes time. Oh, there are moments when we mouth the prayer coin from our lips to God's ear, and that's it—we're done. But generally, the process of praying honest and abandon, with multiple pivots between the two, is just that . . . a process.

There's one final principle to be clear about:

The prayer coin is not magic, nor a formula.

Whispering the words "take this cup, yet not my will" will not manipulate our God into our desires nor shift our will to his. The prayer coin is a conversation with God, with whom we have a relationship.

A prayer for a crisis and for every day, a cumulative and communal prayer, and a prayer of trust, this is a practice that changes us and, through us, changes others.

A Prayer Dare

Now comes the ultimate challenge: choosing to *continually* step into the intimacy promised by the prayer coin practice.

When I'm utterly honest, I have to admit that I've sometimes found myself lackadaisical in my investment in this concept. Of course, I have wrestled in prayer, moving freely from the side of honest to that of abandon, but there are also moments when I realize I'm simply anticipating the pivot from my will to God's. I stand above my own efforts without actually entering them.

Do you know what I mean?

I feel my honest and I imagine my abandon almost as a single act—but at times I don't actually go through the process of either. I hear myself making conclusions for God: *He knows what I'm feeling. I know he loves me. He'll do what's best in the end—for me and those I love.* So I disconnect, jumping to the end result.

Braking hard, forcing myself to focus on what I'm doing, I realize that I'm skipping something God wants to give me. Something that's available only by journeying in and through the process, not just at its end. Not just the *existence* of intimacy but the *experience* of intimacy.

I remember C. S. Lewis somewhere suggesting that God's children satisfy themselves with making mud pies in the slums because they can't imagine making sandcastles on the shore.[2] So true, and that's partly the reason for my lack of effort. But maybe it isn't disbelief so much as a lack of remembering how powerful the results are when I *do* engage. And realizing that God is always waiting for me to do that.

One of my friends describes his struggle with the abandon side of the prayer coin. But each time he slammed into the wall between Take This Cup and Not My Will, he wrote "Even better" in his journal. Why? To help him embrace the fact that what God ultimately offers is far greater than what we could imagine or desire. My friend refused to go rote, instead drumming up an intentional continuation to *experience*. His discovery tutors my indolence.

The prayer coin is a practice we must practice. Rehearse. Apply. Perform. Carry out. No, make that *live* out.

When we practice, it might be that we don't just become better at the prayer coin. As with any discipline—like playing an instrument, picking up golf or tennis or swimming, or speaking a foreign language—we also begin to *enjoy* it more and more.

May we actually commence and then continue a practice that emulates the One who prayed this very prayer: "Take this cup, yet not my will." Because Jesus dared to pray with honest abandon, we can join him and enjoy the intimacy, the alignment with the Father, that he died to provide.

● ● ●

*"The whole desire of our Heavenly Father
is to give Himself to every creature according to
the capacity in which we will receive Him."*
MADAME GUYON[3]

● ● ●

*"I can so understand the two sides
of the prayer coin . . . I'm a musician
and I feel them in music."*
CARLA

CHAPTER 11

Spending the Prayer Coin

"For whoever has will be given more,
and they will have an abundance.
Whoever does not have, even what
they have will be taken from them."
Matthew 25:29

A two-sided coin has been placed in your hands. By God. What will you do with it now?

You've heard the phrase, "Use it or lose it." I think it pretty much sums up Jesus' words in Matthew 25:29.

Need some context?

Near the end of his earthly ministry, in fact at the actual completion of his public teaching, Jesus offered three parables to emphasize that

1. we need to be ready for his return at any time (Matthew 25:1–13),

2. we need to steward what he's given us so that we are ready for his return at any time (Matthew 25:14–30), and

3. we'll all be evaluated in the end by how we
   respond to those around us (Matthew 25:31–46).

Perhaps this is a bit of a simplification, but the parables do make these points.

As we close our consideration of the prayer coin, I want to focus on the second parable: stewarding what God has given us. Our time. Our talents. Our treasures. And our use of one of the most valuable legacies Jesus left—the prayer coin. As I unpack Jesus' words to his followers, both then and now, his meaning is clear. Use it or lose it. Spend it.

Here's how the parable goes:

"Again, it will be like a man going on a journey, who called his servants and entrusted his wealth to them. To one he gave five bags of gold, to another two bags, and to another one bag, each according to his ability. Then he went on his journey. The man who had received five bags of gold went at once and put his money to work and gained five bags more. So also, the one with two bags of gold gained two more. But the man who had received one bag went off, dug a hole in the ground and hid his master's money.

"After a long time the master of those servants returned and settled accounts with them. The man who had received five bags of gold brought the other five. 'Master,' he said, 'you entrusted me with five bags of gold. See, I have gained five more.'

"His master replied, 'Well done, good and faithful servant! You have been faithful with a few things;

I will put you in charge of many things. Come and share your master's happiness!'

"The man with two bags of gold also came. 'Master,' he said, 'you entrusted me with two bags of gold; see, I have gained two more.'

"His master replied, 'Well done, good and faithful servant! You have been faithful with a few things; I will put you in charge of many things. Come and share your master's happiness!'

"Then the man who had received one bag of gold came. 'Master,' he said, 'I knew that you are a hard man, harvesting where you have not sown and gathering where you have not scattered seed. So I was afraid and went out and hid your gold in the ground. See, here is what belongs to you.'

"His master replied, 'You wicked, lazy servant! So you knew that I harvest where I have not sown and gather where I have not scattered seed? Well then, you should have put my money on deposit with the bankers, so that when I returned I would have received it back with interest.

"'So take the bag of gold from him and give it to the one who has ten bags. For whoever has will be given more, and they will have an abundance. Whoever does not have, even what they have will be taken from them. And throw that worthless servant outside, into the darkness, where there will be weeping and gnashing of teeth.'"

I've always been super uncomfortable with the last part of this parable—about darkness, where there's weeping and gnashing of teeth. It sounds so "un-Jesusy," doesn't it? I think Jesus' point here is that God made us to be connected to him in an abiding trust. When we don't trust him, we hold ourselves back from the love we can have in him, the love Jesus died to provide. And when we hold ourselves back from his love, we are left outside, in the dark, in a lonely place, where there is weeping and gnashing of teeth.

But back to the stewardship principle of "use it or lose it." In this parable, the owner—representing God—entrusts three servants with treasure. Two invest their bags of money and make more, which pleases the owner. After all, his ultimate goal is the provision of *abundance*. But one fearful servant buries his treasure. He doesn't invest it; he protects it. Why? From his perspective the master is "hard" (Matthew 25:24) and he was "afraid" (Matthew 25:25). There is something central here: Pure and simple, this man doesn't trust the master. He doesn't use what he's been given, so he loses it.

What happens if we don't spend the prayer coin? If we don't use it, do we lose it?

Kind of.

Let's pause and consider yet another element of this parable. Each bag of gold consists of a "talent," a unit of currency worth about twenty years of a day laborer's wage.[1] Twenty years! The master didn't hand out the "two dimes and a nickel" allowance my mother gave in the 1960s—even adjusted for inflation! No, he entrusted each servant with a huge coinage.

And God has entrusted each of us with the hugely

valuable prayer coin—an exorbitantly expensive concept for him to create.

We began this book with a description of how coins are minted. Imagine melting pure gold and pouring it into forms to create blanks, then using your own strength to hammer the molds and imprint heads and tails on each coin. Real expense and effort are required.

God the Father spared no expense to mint the prayer coin in the life of his Son. And Jesus put the prayer coin into practice, ultimately aligning his will with his Father's. In doing so, he restored the intimacy with God that we were all created to embrace.

When we don't spend the prayer coin, we become like the fearful servant who buried the very treasure God gave him to use. We hold ourselves back from the abundance available in abiding. We abort the whole honest—pivot—abandon—pivot—honest—pivot—abandon process that results in intimacy with the Father. We sit outside in the darkness where there is weeping. And gnashing.

When we don't spend the prayer coin, we miss the intimacy it can buy us.

One of my friends remembers fondly her grand-mother's gift to her each and every Christmas: a lovely, large milk chocolate bar. The first year, Cindy treasured the candy, hiding it deep in a dresser drawer to save for a special time. Except that special time never came. Later, when her mother gave her a summertime chore of cleaning out her drawers, Cindy discovered the chocolate bar in a melty mess. What remained of it was being consumed by ants trailing down her dresser.

Never again, she thought. The next Christmas and every one after, Cindy ate her chocolate bar, enjoying its taste as well as the love her grandmother intended.

I understand Cindy's desire to save her treat. There's such a letdown when we gobble down our holiday goodies, then sit empty-handed, with nothing left to enjoy until the next celebration.

But the prayer coin is a different sort of gift. It offers a unique return.

When we spend it lavishly—on ourselves, on those we love, and on our world—it's never depleted. The prayer coin returns abundance to us. More connection, more alignment, more intimacy with God. "For whoever has will be given more, *and they will have an abundance*" (Matthew 25:29, emphasis added).

What will we do with the prayer coin God has given us? Bury it away to return it to him, unopened and safely encased in its original wrapper? Invest a spin or two in the crisis moments of our days? Palm it in daily devotions, occasionally learning from it but at times unplugging from its true benefit?

Or . . . cash it in toward the end result of *ongoing* intimacy with God? All the time? This has perhaps been my strongest personal takeaway.

I had feared that if I dared go honest, I'd be cosmically zapped, that I'd be forever misunderstood—even rejected. I wasn't. Instead, I was scooped up and held in a safe embrace. Then I assumed I'd be sizzled into abandon—forced to utterly give up my honest desires. In reality, I yielded tender toward God and what I knew he ultimately wanted for me. Instead of being lost in abandon, I was found. Really, the only thing I've given up in this journey is the very fear I was running from.

We need not be afraid. God the Father has given us an incredible gift—the prayer that Jesus himself prayed in the garden of Gethsemane. Like Jesus, we can be honest with the Father. Like Jesus, we can pray with abandon. Like Jesus, we can pivot, back and forth as many times as it takes to align our wills with God's. And, like Jesus, we can enjoy total intimacy with the Father.

Spend the prayer coin lavishly, with the currency of both sides: honest and abandon. It will always come back to us in the ultimate profit—a closer relationship with the One who spent all for us.

• • •

"I have come that they might have life,
and that they may have it more abundantly."
—JESUS, JOHN 10:10 NKJV

The Gospel Passages

Matthew 26:36–46

Then Jesus went with his disciples to a place called Gethsemane, and he said to them, "Sit here while I go over there and pray." He took Peter and the two sons of Zebedee along with him, and he began to be sorrowful and troubled. Then he said to them, "My soul is overwhelmed with sorrow to the point of death. Stay here and keep watch with me."

Going a little farther, he fell with his face to the ground and prayed, "My Father, if it is possible, may this cup be taken from me. Yet not as I will, but as you will."

Then he returned to his disciples and found them sleeping. "Couldn't you men keep watch with me for one hour?" he asked Peter. "Watch and pray so that you will not fall into temptation. The spirit is willing, but the flesh is weak."

He went away a second time and prayed, "My Father, if it is not possible for this cup to be taken away unless I drink it, may your will be done."

When he came back, he again found them sleeping, because their eyes were heavy. So he left them and went away once more and prayed the third time, saying the same thing.

Then he returned to the disciples and said to them, "Are you still sleeping and resting? Look, the hour has come, and the Son of Man is delivered into the hands of sinners. Rise! Let us go! Here comes my betrayer!"

Mark 14:32–42

They went to a place called Gethsemane, and Jesus said to his disciples, "Sit here while I pray." He took Peter, James and John along with him, and he began to be deeply distressed and troubled. "My soul is over-whelmed with sorrow to the point of death," he said to them. "Stay here and keep watch."

Going a little farther, he fell to the ground and prayed that if possible the hour might pass from him. "Abba, Father," he said, "everything is possible for you. Take this cup from me. Yet not what I will, but what you will."

Then he returned to his disciples and found them sleeping. "Simon," he said to Peter, "are you asleep? Couldn't you keep watch for one hour? Watch and pray so that you will not fall into temptation. The spirit is willing, but the flesh is weak."

Once more he went away and prayed the same thing. When he came back, he again found them sleeping, because their eyes were heavy. They did not know what to say to him.

Returning the third time, he said to them, "Are you still sleeping and resting? Enough! The hour has come.

Look, the Son of Man is delivered into the hands of sinners. Rise! Let us go! Here comes my betrayer!"

Luke 22:39–46

Jesus went out as usual to the Mount of Olives, and his disciples followed him. On reaching the place, he said to them, "Pray that you will not fall into temptation." He withdrew about a stone's throw beyond them, knelt down and prayed, "Father, if you are willing, take this cup from me; yet not my will, but yours be done." An angel from heaven appeared to him and strengthened him. And being in anguish, he prayed more earnestly, and his sweat was like drops of blood falling to the ground.

When he rose from prayer and went back to the disciples, he found them asleep, exhausted from sorrow. "Why are you sleeping?" he asked them. "Get up and pray so that you will not fall into temptation."

John 18:1–11

When he had finished praying, Jesus left with his disciples and crossed the Kidron Valley. On the other side there was a garden, and he and his disciples went into it.

Now Judas, who betrayed him, knew the place, because Jesus had often met there with his disciples. So Judas came to the garden, guiding a detachment of soldiers and some officials from the chief priests and the Pharisees. They were carrying torches, lanterns and weapons.

Jesus, knowing all that was going to happen to him, went out and asked them, "Who is it you want?"

"Jesus of Nazareth," they replied.

"I am he," Jesus said. (And Judas the traitor was standing there with them.) When Jesus said, "I am he," they drew back and fell to the ground.

Again he asked them, "Who is it you want?"

"Jesus of Nazareth," they said.

Jesus answered, "I told you that I am he. If you are looking for me, then let these men go." This happened so that the words he had spoken would be fulfilled: "I have not lost one of those you gave me."

Then Simon Peter, who had a sword, drew it and struck the high priest's servant, cutting off his right ear. (The servant's name was Malchus.)

Jesus commanded Peter, "Put your sword away! Shall I not drink the cup the Father has given me?"

The Prayer Coin
Study Guide

SESSION ONE:
Our Problems with Prayer *(Chapter 1)*

1. On a scale of 1 to 10 (with 1 being non-existent and 10 being thriving in closeness to God), how would you rank your prayer life?

2. What kind of prayer problems do you experience?

3. Can you think back to a time when prayer was more fulfilling in your life? What were your circumstances then?

4. Read Matthew 6:5–15, 7:7–12 and Luke 11:1–13, 18:1–8. What does Jesus teach us about how to pray in these passages?

5. What, according to Luke 22:42, are the two sides of Jesus' garden prayer?

6. Consider Elisa's summary of the two sides of prayer: honest and abandon (see page 16). Which is most familiar to you? Why?

7. Read Chapter 1, "Our Problems with Prayer," and underline the quotations. Read them aloud. Which resonate with you, and why?

8. As a result of your study of the prayer coin, what would you like to see change in your prayer life?

9. Obtain a journal and label the left side of a page Take This Cup (Honest) and the right side Not My Will (Abandon). Pick a topic of tug-of-war in your own prayer life, and begin the prayer coin journey.

10. In preparation for the next session, read Chapters 1, 2, and 3.

SESSION TWO:
The Two-Sided Prayer *(Chapters 2–3)*

1. Scripture shows that Jesus prayed like no one else— what were some aspects of his prayer life? (See John 4:32; Luke 3:21, 5:16, 9:29; Mark 1:35–36, 6:46.)

2. On page 26, Elisa describes the setting for Jesus' garden prayer. Why do you think he chose Gethsemane for this important night of wrestling in prayer? (See Luke 22:39; John 18:2.)

3. Take time to read the four gospel accounts of Jesus' two-sided prayer (Matthew 26:36–46; Mark 14:32–42; Luke 22:39–46; and John 18:1–11—either in your own Bible or in *The Prayer Coin*, pages 171–74). What do you discover as you review the four tellings? What words are included in each of the accounts? Why do you think that's important?

4. Wrestle with the phrases "take this cup" and "not my will." They can be paraphrased "what I want" and "what God wants." Which side are you more apt to pray—honest or abandon? Why?

5. On page 29, Elisa reports Max Lucado's observation as he prepared to preach on two verses in the psalms requested for a funeral. How does his impression affect you?

6. Describe Jesus' invitation to his first-century followers recorded in Matthew 26:36 and Mark 14:32. What was he inviting them to do?

7. Read Matthew 26:37–38 and Mark 14:33–34 to see Jesus' invitation to Peter, James, and John. How does John 15:1–11 explain Jesus' intent for his disciples?

8. Why would Jesus tell his disciples to pray that they don't fall into temptation (Matthew 26:41; Mark 14:38; Luke 22:40)?

9. What do you think it meant for the first-century disciples to see Jesus praying the two-sided prayer of honest and abandon? What does it mean for us today?

10. Go to your prayer coin journal and continue recording your two-sided prayer discoveries. In preparation for the next session, read Chapters 4 and 5.

SESSION THREE:

Honest *(Chapters 4-5)*

1. On pages 70–76, Elisa tells the story about how children are honest until they learn not to be. Can you remember the first time you tried dishonesty? What were the circumstances? Why did you make that choice? What happened as a result?

2. What is the "cup" that Jesus was destined to drink? (See Psalm 75:8; Isaiah 51:17; Jeremiah 25:15; Isaiah 52:13–53:12; 2 Corinthians 5:21; Hebrews 2:10, 5:7–10.)

3. As a result of Jesus drinking the cup of suffering, the cup of life and love and restoration could be offered for us all. How does the Bible describe this? (See Psalm 16:5, 23:5, 116:13; 1 Corinthians 10:16.)

4. Read John 12:27 and Mark 14:35. How could Jesus ask the Father to remove the cup when it was the very reason he'd come to earth?

5. Each gospel writer expresses Jesus' Take This Cup plea a bit differently:
   - "My Father, if it is possible . . ." (Matthew 26:39).
   - "My Father, if it is not possible . . . unless I drink it . . ." (Matthew 26:42).
   - . . . if possible the hour pass might pass . . . (Mark 14:35).
   - "Abba, Father . . . everything is possible for you . . ." (Mark 14:36).

- "Father, if you are willing . . ." (Luke 22:42).
  Why might this be?

6. Read aloud pages 57–58 and pause to truly consider the heart that prayed "take this cup." Is there one element that touches you uniquely today? Why?

7. Read Hebrews 5:7. How does this description of Jesus' suffering offer insight into his honest plea, "Take this cup"?

8. Sometimes praying "take this cup" means "give me what I want, God" and sometimes it means "take away what I don't want." What honest Take This Cup prayer are you currently praying?

9. As you consider your own Take This Cup prayer, what might hold you back from complete honesty?

10. Continue your prayer journal. How has this week's lesson on "honest" deepened your expression of Take This Cup in your journal? In preparation for the next session, read Chapters 6 and 7.

Abandon (Chapters 6-7)

1. On pages 93–94, Elisa struggles to define the second side of the prayer coin. Recall the various terms she originally suggested: *surrender*, *relinquish*, *submit*. What does each word mean? Why does Elisa settle on the concept of "abandon"? How does this concept sit with you?

2. Consider this statement: Abandon is a choice. Read Philippians 2:1–8. How does this passage of the apostle Paul explain how Jesus was able to pray in abandon, "not my will"?

3. Now consider this statement: Abandon comes from love. On page 99, Elisa traces the logic that moves Jesus from honest to abandon. Read the list of Scriptures out loud, and consider how Jesus reviewed what he knew about his Father and their relationship.

4. Finally, consider this statement: Abandon grows from obedience. Read Hebrews 5:7–8. How did Jesus "grow in obedience"?

5. Elisa discusses the concept of "auto-abandon" on page 107. Do you ever slip into auto-abandon? Why would we?

6. For many reasons, we avoid abandon: We might think God wants to hurt us. We might disbelieve his love. We might even have concluded that God is not good. Using your prayer coin journal, ask yourself each day this week just why you might tend to avoid abandon. Create a list of the lies that tell you abandon is unwise.

7. The way forward in abandon, to embracing what God wants rather than what we want, is taken in "baby steps." Again, using your prayer coin journal, create God's answers to the lies you've been cataloguing. What baby steps might you take to stop avoiding abandon and instead move toward it?

8. What current issue are you struggling to abandon to God?

9. Reread Richard Foster's quote on page 116. What are the "gains" of abandon?

10. Continue your prayer journal. How has this week's lesson on abandon deepened your expression of Not My Will in your journal? In preparation for the next session, read Chapters 8 and 9.

SESSION FIVE:
Pivot *(Chapters 8–9)*

1. Define the word *pivot*. How does it apply to the prayer coin?

2. Read Luke 22:39–46 and Hebrews 5:7. What role do you think God's "answers" played in Jesus' pivot between honest and abandon—between Take This Cup and Not My Will?

3. Read John 18:1–11. Why do you think John included only an allusion to Jesus' two-sided prayer coin rather than the prayer itself?

4. Jesus' words in John 15–17 offer insight into his ultimate goal for believers: that we be one as he and the Father are one. Read John 17:11, 20–23. How might this actually be Jesus' ultimate goal in praying the prayer coin?

5. On pages 129–130, Elisa describes how the pivot of intimacy results in alignment. What is the difference between submission and alignment?

6. Review the process of how the third side of a coin—the edge—is formed on page 130. How does this third side help you understand the process of Jesus' pivot between honest and abandon?

7. On page 125, Elisa says, "Prayer creates honesty which develops trust and results in surrender." How does the pivot of the prayer coin express this process?

8. If Jesus' goal is that we be one as he and the Father are one, and if he invites us into the process of the prayer coin with him, how can we learn to pivot as he did between the two sides?

9. Elisa tells the story of her howling dogs on pages 143–146. How does this story help you see God's longing for you? How does God's longing draw you closer to him?

10. In your prayer coin journal, try to let each *honest* pivot you into a new *abandon*—and then allow the revealed *abandon* send you into a new *honest*. Review pages 139–140 for examples. In preparation for the next session, read Chapters 10 and 11.

SESSION SIX:
The Prayer Coin Practice *(Chapters 10–11)*

1. Before beginning this last session, take some time to read back through your prayer coin journal. Look for discoveries as well as struggles and ongoing questions. Carry them forward into this session.

2. The prayer coin practice often begins as a crisis prayer. What motivated you to pick up this book and begin this study? Was it a crisis? If so, what has occurred as a result of your own practice?

3. The prayer coin practice is also an everyday prayer. How often do you find yourself praying the prayer coin? Why do you think this is the case?

4. On pages 155–156, Elisa suggests that this prayer is a cumulative prayer. What does she mean by that? How do you see it layering each time you pray it?

5. If you are doing this study in a group, choose a subject and try praying this prayer together: go around the circle, each praying in turn and working together to layer honest, pivot to abandon, then back to honest, and so on. What do you discover as you pray communally?

6. Prayer involves trust, and the prayer coin can build trust as we keep praying it. Can you identify some areas where your trust has been challenged by this prayer? Where the prayer has built trust?

7. Is it tempting to view the prayer coin as a formula? How can we avoid this way of thinking?

8. Read Matthew 25:14–30. Consider how spending the prayer coin (as opposed to burying it) might influence your life. How might spending or burying the prayer coin influence the lives of others around you?

9. What might God want to give to you as you "spend" the prayer coin in your days?

10. On page 167, Elisa summarized the premise of the prayer coin, saying:

> Imagine melting pure gold and pouring it into forms to create blanks, then using your own strength to hammer the molds and imprint heads and tails on each coin. Real expense and effort are required.
>
> God the Father spared no expense to mint the prayer coin in the life of his Son. And Jesus put the prayer coin into practice, ultimately aligning his will with his Father's. In doing so, he restored the intimacy with God that we were all created to embrace.

Having read this summary, ask God to help you understand where and how you might spend the prayer coin.

• • •

Visit theprayercoin.org
for more resources
and to share what you've learned.

Acknowledgments

I didn't really think I'd write another book. And especially not a book on prayer. As I shared in chapter one, I don't view myself as some kind of prayer warrior equipped to guide others into deeper conversation with God. But, really, that *is* what I am. We all are. Because of the intimacy Jesus died to provide for us, we can *all* converse with God in honest abandon.

The prayer coin is teaching me this reality. And I have many to thank for both recognizing its power and learning to practice its offering.

So . . . thanks to:

Miranda, Ken, and Paul at Discovery House. You challenged me to write a "big book." It may not be *large*, but the concept is life-changingly "big."

John, Cathy, Heather, Julie, and team at Our Daily Bread Ministries, for all your brilliant marketing, cover, and curriculum efforts to supplement the message of the prayer coin and share it with readers.

Brian, Bill, Daniel, and Mart at *Discover the Word*, for your grace in giving me space to write the book rather than create radio programs, and for allowing me to try out the material on air well before the manuscript was quite formed.

Bryan at Alive Communications and Joy at the Frontline Group for your faithful feedback in forming both words and presentation for this message to increase the reach of the concept.

Colorado Community Church in Aurora, Colorado, for responding to my "New Year's Prayer Dare," joining in with comments about your own discoveries as you practiced the prayer coin.

My many friends who read and reread and practiced and learned the prayer coin in their own lives: Karen, Carol, Carla, Cindy, J'Anne, Debbie, Carla, Evan, Mart, Bill, Craig, and especially Steve, for allowing me a peek inside your prayer coin closet.

My family—always supportive and sweetly proud of my efforts.

And most of all, to my husband, Evan, for your selfless giving over of this personal discovery to allow me to form it for others. Your recognition of Jesus' two-sided sentence, handed to me to explore, study, and then share, will change many, many lives. Mine included. (PS, thanks for getting sick when you did too—that whole ordeal made the prayer coin so *real*!)

Notes

CHAPTER 1: Our Problems with Prayer

1. Paul Miller, "The Hardest Place in the World to Pray," April 11, 2017, https://thedisciplemaker.org/the-hardest-place-in-the-world -to-pray/

2. Richard Foster, *Prayer: Finding the Heart's True Home* (New York: HarperCollins, 2003), xi–xii.

3. Max Lucado, *Before Amen: The Power of a Simple Prayer* (Nashville: Thomas Nelson, 2014), 2–3.

4. Tim Keller, *Prayer: Experiencing Awe and Intimacy with God* (New York: Dutton, 2014), 18.

CHAPTER 2: Jesus' Two-Sided Prayer

1. Richard Rohr, *Everything Belongs: The Gift of Contemplative Prayer* (New York: The Crossroad Publishing Company, 1999), 93.

2. D. A. Carson, *The Gospel according to John* (Leicester, England; Apollos, an imprint of Inter-Varsity Press, 1991), 576–577.

3. D. A. Carson, *NIV Zondervan Study Bible* (Grand Rapids, Michigan: Zondervan, 2015), 2050.

4. J. P. Lange and J. J. van Oosterzee, translated by P. Schaff and C. C. Starbuck, *A Commentary on the Holy Scriptures: Luke.* (Bellingham, Washington: Logos Bible Software, 2008), 349.

5. Lucado, *Before Amen*, 46.

6. For more on Mary of Bethany, see Elisa Morgan, *She Did What She Could* (Chicago: Tyndale, 2009).

7. Alexandre Dumas, *The Count of Monte Cristo* (New York: Bantam Books, 1956), 34.

CHAPTER 3: **Our Two-Sided Prayer**

1. Francis Frangipane, *Holiness, Truth, and the Presence of God* (Lake Mary, Florida: Strang Publications, 1986), 75.

2. Keller, 230.

3. Philip Yancey, *Prayer: Does It Make Any Difference?* (Grand Rapids, Michigan: Zondervan, 2006), 17.

CHAPTER 4: **Jesus' Honest—***Take This Cup*

1. Foster, 134.

2. Lucado, *Before Amen*, 13.

3. Joachim Jeremias, *The Prayers of Jesus* (Philadelphia: SCM, 1967), 111.

4. "Holding hands to comfort loved ones does help reduce pain, US study shows," June 23, 2017, http://www.telegraph.co.uk/news/2017/06/23/holding-hands-comfort-loved-ones-does-help-reduce-pain-us-study/.

5. Darrell Bock, *Baker Exegetical Commentary on the New Testament: Luke, Volume 2* (Grand Rapids, Michigan: Baker Books, 1996), 1758.

6. Carson, *NIV Zondervan Study Bible*, 2130.

7. R. C. H. Lenski, *The Interpretation of St. Luke's Gospel* (Minneapolis: Augsburg Publishing House, 1961), 1075–1077. Logos.

8. Bock, 1761.

9. Lenski, 1075–1077.

10. C. S. Lewis, *Letters to Malcolm, Chiefly on Prayer* (New York: HarperCollins, 1963), 111.

CHAPTER 5: **Our Honest—***Take This Cup*

1. Keller, 237.

2. C. S. Lewis, *A Grief Observed* (New York: Bantam Books, 1963), 34–35.

3. Lewis, *Letters to Malcolm*, 27.

4. Shauna Niequist, *Present Over Perfect: Leaving Behind Frantic*

for a Simpler, More Soulful Way of Living (Grand Rapids, Michigan: Zondervan, 2016), 75.

5. Max Lucado, *You'll Get Through This* (Nashville: Thomas Nelson, 2013), 29.

6. Margaret Feinberg, *The Sacred Echo* (Grand Rapids, Michigan: Zondervan, 2008), 26.

7. Sherry Harney with Kevin Harney, *Praying with Eyes Wide Open: A Life-Changing Way to Talk with God* (Grand Rapids, Michigan: Baker Books, 2017), 134.

8. Anne Lamott, *Help, Thanks, Wow: The Three Essential Prayers* (New York: Riverhead Books, 2013), 3–5.

9. Yancey, 42.

10. Brene Brown, *Daring Greatly* (New York: Gotham, 2012), 32–56.

11. Curt Thompson, *The Soul of Shame* (Downer's Grove, Illinois: IVP Books, 2015), 121–22.

12. Thompson, 123.

13. Harney, 127.

CHAPTER 6: **Jesus' Abandon**—*Not My Will*

1. https://www.merriam-webster.com/dictionary/abandon.

2. Carson, *NIV Zondervan Study Bible,* 2051.

3. Lenski, 1073–1074.

4. Keller, 80.

5. R. C. Sproul, *Does Prayer Change Things?* (Lake Mary, Florida: Reformation Trust, 1984), 1.

6. Andrew Murray, *With Christ in the School of Prayer* (Springdale, Pennsylvania: Whitaker House, 1981), 211–212.

CHAPTER 7: **Our Abandon**—*Not My Will*

1. Mark Batterson, *The Circle Maker: Praying Circles around Your Biggest Dreams and Greatest Fears* (Grand Rapids, Michigan: Zondervan, 2011), 14.

2. Lewis, *A Grief Observed*, 79.

3. Foster, 47.

4. Keller, 238–239.

5. Ann Voskamp, *The Broken Way: A Daring Path into the Abundant Life* (Grand Rapids, Michigan: Zondervan, 2016), 99–100.

6. Lamott, 5.

7. Foster, 53.

8. Richard Rohr, "The Cross," Center for Action and Contemplation, April 28, 2017, https://cac.org/suffering-love-2017-04-28/.

9. Foster, 266–267.

10. Foster, 72.

11. Patricia Raybon, *I Told the Mountain to Move*, (Chicago: SaltRiver, 2005), 232–233.

12. Leslie Montgomery, *Redemptive Suffering* (Wheaton, Illinois: Crossway Books, 2006), 25.

CHAPTER 8: **Jesus' Pivot**—*The Space Between Honest and Abandon*

1. Yancey, 233.

2. Keller, 238.

3. Matthew Henry, *Commentary on the Whole Bible: Complete and Unabridged in One Volume* (Peabody, Massachusetts: Hendrickson, 1994), 1903. Logos.

4. Lenski, 1075–77.

5. John D. Grassmick in John F. Walvoord and Roy B. Zuck, editors, *The Bible Knowledge Commentary: An Exposition of the Scriptures by Dallas Seminary Faculty*, Vol. 2 (Colorado Springs: David C. Cook), 180.

6. Carson, *The Gospel according to John*, 579.

7. J. P. Louw and E. A. Nida, *Greek-English Lexicon of the New Testament: Based on Semantic Domains, Volume 1* (New York: United Bible Societies, 1996), 398.